Getting on with Kids
in Secondary Schools

D1386024

15.95

To my precious wife Susie
who has given me the time,
space and love needed for me
to write this book.

Getting on with Kids in Secondary Schools

How to establish and maintain good working relationships with your pupils

Gererd Dixie

Illustrations by Audrey Percy

Peter Francis Publishers

Peter Francis Publishers
The Old School House
Little Fransham
Dereham
Norfolk NR19 2JP UK

© Gererd Dixie 2005 (text)
© Audrey Percy 2005 (illustrations)

A CIP catalogue record for this book is available from the British Library

ISBN 1-870167-42-2

Printed and bound in Great Britain
by Biddles Ltd, King's Lynn

Contents

Acknowledgements

A debt of gratitude to my 'little' big sister Teresa Edge who lovingly and painstakingly edited this book

To my dear friend and colleague Katy Wilks for her editorial help and unflagging support

To Audrey Percy (alpercy2004@yahoo.co.uk) for her wonderful and insightful illustrations

One looks back with appreciation to the brilliant teachers, but with gratitude to those who touched our human feeling. The curriculum is so much necessary raw material, but warmth is the vital element for the growing plant and for the soul of the child. (Carl Jung, 1875-1961)

Chapter 1

Introduction

B efore you start flicking through these pages to check whether you think it is worth reading this book, I feel I should convey this important message. As a teacher with over thirty years of experience, I fully understand the rigours and stresses of the job. At times you have so many demands placed upon you that you simply do not know which way to turn. The last thing a busy and stressed teacher needs is to have to wade through pages and pages of theoretical jargon about what he or she should be doing in the classroom. This book, therefore, has been written with *real* youngsters, *real* teachers and realistic classroom scenarios in mind. Although it may have an academic flavour in places, it has been written primarily as a down to earth practical guide to establishing, maintaining and developing good working relationships with your pupils. Having said this, I am going to break my rule just once and describe to you a piece of academic research that has done more to shape my teaching career than anything else. The relevance and context of this research will be revealed as you make your journey through the book.

Zimpher and Howey (1987) described four types of teacher competence which they believed were critical to effective teaching, and which I feel all teachers should know about. These are technical, clinical, critical and personal competences, the details of each of which have been outlined overleaf.

Teachers display *technical* competence when they

- determine *what* is to be learned;
- determine *how* it is to be learned;
- employ the criteria by which success is to be measured;
- show mastery of methods of instruction, for example, specific skills such as how to ask good questions;
- apply appropriate teaching strategies;
- select and organise appropriate resources;
- structure the classroom for learning;
- employ techniques that are successful in helping to establish and maintain good classroom discipline.

Teachers display *clinical* competence when they

- adopt the role of a problem-solver and clinician who is able to frame and solve practical problems through the process of reflective action and inquiry;
- set up and test hypotheses in the classroom, and solve such problems as what should be done about disruptive pupil behaviour, or what the best format for group work should be;
- take on the role of action researcher, exploring the extent to which the various learning theories match the realities of classroom life.

Teachers display *critical* competence when they

- adopt a critical role of the education system by looking at such issues as the social conditions of schooling, and the influence of the hidden curriculum;
- explore the power and authority bases both within and outside the school;
- ask questions about the basic ideology of schools, about the nature of society in general, and about the effects of negative socialisation on the teaching process;
- ask other questions that present a more critical and radical notion of the structures of schools.

Teachers display *personal* competence when they

- use themselves as effective and humane instruments of class-room instruction;
- use their intra-personal skills to confront themselves critically and develop their levels of self-awareness;
- understand fully the interactive nature of teaching by show-ing an awareness of the role of verbal and non-verbal symbols in the teaching process;
- understand how small group processes work;
- use their good inter-personal skills to create a warm and supportive learning environment.

Although all these competences are important, if you aspire to be a highly successful teacher, you need to make sure that you are not over-reliant on one particular domain. You must, therefore, adopt a more considered and balanced approach towards your teaching role. Although most pupils are not fully able to articulate the prerequisites of a good teacher, I am convinced that they do ask a number of quite searching internal questions about the person standing in front of them. My research into pupil/teacher relationships, together with my lengthy teaching experience, has shown me that pupils *do* see good teachers as being able both to control their classes, make their teaching spaces purposeful and create effective scenarios for learning. They *do* want their teachers to reflect on the things that work and do not work in the classroom; they *do* want the teacher to understand how their home backgrounds and family situations affect their work in school.

The other really important point for me to make is that these four competences do not exist in isolation, since teachers have many roles in school. It is virtually impossible to put these into nice neat categor-ies. I am aware that all these roles overlap and are equally important in their own right, but I am going to focus mainly on the *personal* and *technical* competences here. These contribute most to the making of the type of teacher who can build good working relationships with their pupils. This surely has got to be the principle aim of any successful teacher. Without such relationships effective learning will simply not take place. This book recognises the importance of the establishment of a successful partnership between teacher and pupil and offers guid-ance and advice on how this partnership can be fully realised.

Who is the book for and why has it been written?

As a professional development tutor, I have made numerous local education authority (LEA) and school-based presentations to initial teacher training (ITT) students, newly qualified teachers and teachers still in the dawn of their careers. The teachers in all of these groups I call 'beginning' teachers. Feedback from these sessions, as well as from numerous individual mentoring sessions with them, has shown me quite clearly the need for a book such as this. These teachers want to know why they experience behavioural, learning and relational problems with specific youngsters in their classes, when the very same pupils seem to be able to strike up good working relationships with other teachers in the school. It is a source of great frustration to them that, no matter what they seem to do to try to redress these issues, things do not apparently get any better for them as far as their relationships with these pupils are concerned.

So, why is this book necessary? The interactive nature of teaching means that the establishment and maintenance of good working relationships with pupils lie at the very heart of good discipline and effective learning. The strategies required for teachers to gain effective classroom control are often covered in depth in the Postgraduate Certificate in Education (PGCE) courses. Monitoring and assessment issues are also given a great deal of attention. Any weaknesses in subject knowledge can be compensated for by teachers carrying out individual research and/or through their experiences of having to teach unfamiliar units of work. However, the issue of teacher/pupil relationships is often not given the focus it deserves. Although there seems to be a substantial amount of literature dealing with whole-class behavioural issues, I am convinced that there is a need for a book that focuses on the importance of teacher/pupil relationships in the learning equation. It is my belief that good teacher/pupil relationships lie at the very heart of quality learning. Although this book has been written with beginning teachers in mind, I feel confident that it will benefit any practising teacher, irrespective of their age or position on the career ladder. I also believe that this publication should be on the shelves of all professional development tutors who will be able to use the mass of realistic exemplar scenarios and exercises for their school based in-service sessions.

What is in this book?

This book is divided into eight chapters, each focusing on distinct areas relevant to the core issue, that of establishing, maintaining and developing good learning relationships between teachers and pupils.

Through the medium of free-response questionnaires, Chapter 2 briefly explores a number of adult memories of teachers. The purpose of this chapter is to raise the reader's awareness of the impact teachers can have on our lives, right into adult life. Through a discussion of the various traits and characteristics of effective teachers, this chapter offers the reader some excellent role models of good teaching. The latter part of the chapter describes some of the bad memories which respondents have had of their teachers and then goes on to explore the effects that these have in later years.

Bearing in mind that teaching is very much a two-way process and that real learning depends largely upon successful pupil-teacher relationships, it is very important for teachers to reflect constructively on their practice. Chapter 3 asks the question: 'What sort of teacher are you?' Through the use of an audit, the reader will be given the opportunity to analyse and evaluate their own traits and characteristics, and to explore the effects that these may have on their relationships with the pupils in their classes.

The initial part of Chapter 4 looks briefly at the creation of a market in education, and focuses on the need for teachers to gain an understanding of how their work is perceived by pupils. The chapter goes on to offer some research findings that describe a range of pupil perceptions of their teachers, before finally exploring the possible implications of perceptions such as these on our teaching.

Chapter 5 shows how being a good classroom manager, and how creating a positive classroom climate, can really enhance the quality of relationships between teacher and pupil and, as a result, improve the learning scenarios in school. Much of the advice and guidance offered within this chapter will be presented through an exploration of brain-based learning.

Much has been said in the media about the poor behaviour of some pupils in schools. Chapter 6 describes some of the characteristics of this anti-social behaviour before going on to explore a number of possible reasons behind the actions of disaffected pupils. It builds on the previous chapter by offering strategies and guidance designed to build good working relationships with those disaffected pupils for whom whole-class management plans have failed.

Perhaps the most demanding role for all practising teachers is that of being a form tutor. Chapter 7 provides advice and guidance on how to be a successful, effective and popular form tutor. The chapter describes ways in which teachers can provide formal and informal opportunities for the personal and social development of their pupils. It then goes on to suggest how to create an infrastructure that will support the school's ethos on behaviour and attitudes. The chapter concludes by exploring ways in which teachers can support the academic progress of their pupils and also act as an efficient conduit for communications between school and home.

How to use this book

You might like to read this book from cover to cover in order to get an overall picture of the themes, issues and recommended practices explored in each chapter. Alternatively, since each chapter stands on its own, you may wish to turn to a specific chapter to explore a particular issue that is relevant to your needs.

Finally, it is important for me to make it clear that references to individual teachers and situations in this book have been changed to ensure that anonymity has been maintained.

Chapter 2

No One Forgets a Good Teacher

Between 2000 and 2001, the Teacher Training Agency ran an inspirational campaign entitled: *No one forgets a good teacher*. This recruiting message was conveyed extensively on cinema and television screens, and on billboards across Great Britain, inspiring me,

and thousands like me, to consider my own recollections of teachers. The fundamental question we were all asking at the time was: What were the magic ingredients that brought these teachers so fondly to the forefront of our thoughts? I am confident that this chapter will provide you with some of the answers.

Whenever I reminisce about my distant school-days, I do not immediately recall the subject matter we covered in lessons. My mind does not leap to questions such as who won the Battle of Waterloo, what exactly Pythagoras had to offer, or why the flood plains of rivers are so important. Crucial though these topics are, they do not provide a major focus for my memories. Instead, I start to reminisce about the *way* I was taught and about those teachers who took the time and trouble to get to know me. I think fondly of those teachers who managed to inspire me, make me laugh, think, and, above all, make me care about myself and about our world. Unfortunately, as far as my own school experiences were concerned, these teachers were few and far between. My memories of my school days are at best clouded and at worst, unhappy. It is fair to say that my academic, social and emotional development took place long after I had left school. Any success I have had is down to a combination of latent ability, being in the right place at the right time, encouragement from those dear to me, and a lot of self-motivation and determination on my part. How I wish *my* teachers had read this job description in the prospectus of a leading teacher training university:

A good teacher is:

- Energetic
- A good communicator
- Able to inspire and enthuse
- Enjoys working with young people
- A good manager of resources, material and time
- Imaginative and creative – and has a sense of humour!

Teaching is a demanding career, physically, emotionally and intellectually. It calls for energy, dedication, patience and enthusiasm. You must have enthusiasm for your subject, and, far more important, you must be able to form a relationship with and control the class. Class management skills are essential. You also need to be able to think on your feet. This is not a nine-to-five job. There will be a lot of preparation and marking to do in the evenings and weekends. There are also exams to prepare, invigilate and mark. All this calls for good time management, self-discipline, administration and organisational skills as well as good supervisory and leadership skills. (University of Kent, Careers Advisory Service, 2004)

Or you may want to consider looking at this guidance information published by an online employment agency, which offered this brief but, nonetheless, pithy job description of the requirements of a good teacher.

What skills and abilities do I need?

It sounds basic but it is essential you like and relate well to kids! A good teacher will be committed to opening up young minds. You'll also need excellent communication skills, a keen intellect, creativity and bags of energy. It also helps to have a sense of humour. (The Potential Job Board Company Ltd, 2004)

Let's face it, if you were taught by teachers who met all these criteria you would most certainly remember them, wouldn't you? Just think of the impact these teachers would have made in increasing your motivation levels and in providing you with the knowledge, skills, values and attitudes required for you to live a successful and happy life.

I have briefly described experiences of my own school days to you but what I want to do is to furnish you with a number of different memories from other teachers. To gain these, I issued questionnaires to the 170 members of the teaching and non-teaching staff in two local secondary schools. Their brief was simple. I wanted these people to recount their memories of their primary and/or secondary school teachers. The response was simply overwhelming, both in terms of the written replies given to me, and also in the amount of discussion and experience-sharing the process initiated. It was obvious that in asking this question, I had really hit a nerve! I could not walk down the corridor without someone wanting to talk to me about their early school experiences. So why have I included the results in the book? What is the relevance of these findings to the core purpose of this publication? The answer to these questions is simple. I feel that there is much to be learned from the reflections of adults on their childhood days in schools, especially if those adults are teachers! What became absolutely apparent at a very early stage in the research was how important teachers are in the formative stages of our lives. Therefore, you, as beginning teachers, should cast your minds back to your own school days. Think about the characteristics of those teachers who inspired you, and those teachers who lacked the ability to motivate you. You will then be able to use these memories to good effect when building relationships with your own pupils. However, let me get one thing straight. I am not suggesting that you simply become carbon copies of your heroes – something that would be both inappropriate and unrealistic. However, I do feel that whilst on our journey through life we both consciously and unconsciously select, and take on, many of the characteristics of the people we admire, and these gradually become subsumed into our personality. Providing a teacher recreates these characteristics in a style of his or her own I see nothing wrong with this. What is important for beginning teachers to note is that they need to become their *own people* as soon as possible – pupils will respect them for this.

I found it fascinating to read through the results of this low level primary research. Processing this material, however, was quite difficult. Because of the *emotional* nature of this issue and because I wanted to obtain a high degree of validity in my findings, I decided to use a free-response style questionnaire to elicit thoughts, feelings and emotions. Although the results were highly relevant and useful, many of the responses were free-flowing and somewhat lacking in focus and were, therefore, quite difficult to categorise. As you will see below I used three broad categories to describe respondents' experiences.

Motivation, enthusiasm, interest in the individual and encouragement

In virtually all the responses made by the sample research population, there was some reference made to the teacher's enthusiasm for their subject, their encouragement and interest in the individual, and their sheer passion for teaching. In order to capture the flavour of my findings I have included a number of extracts from their responses.

'I remember him because of his sheer enthusiasm for everything he did. Obviously he was heavily involved in school sports and he was very encouraging towards me.'

'My favourite teacher showed enthusiasm and a love of their subject – you aspired to be like them.'

'Mr X opened my eyes to media studies and I have always said that it is down to him that I now teach this subject. He had a passion for media, and most of the information he gave us had come from his own research, not textbooks, and I really admired him for that. He opened my eyes to new films and ideas, which I surprised myself by liking them ... I remember him today mostly because when I plan for lessons for new topics I always think about how he'd do it. If I can imagine him teaching my lesson, I know it's right.'

'Geography was never really a subject that I would have said that I actually *enjoyed* until I had this teacher. As a result of his lessons my perception was altered and I went on to do geography A Level (the subject I got my best A Level grade in!) I always knew how hard the teacher worked for us and in return I always ensured I worked equally hard. The teacher's enthusiasm for the subject really inspired me and made me want to learn ... this is the teacher that made me want to enter the profession – I hope that I am able to inspire pupils in the same way.'

'Mr X was my history teacher for GCSE and A Level. He was enthusiastic and knew a lot of stuff! He made the subject relevant and exciting to study ... He made me see that history is the most important subject in the world – to understand human nature, decisions, events and to make sense of the world in which we live. He *inspired* me to learn and to become a teacher.'

'My favourite teacher at secondary school was Mrs X who taught me English ... the interest and enthusiasm she exuded prompted my enthusiasm and when I pondered on becoming an English teacher, I thought of her.'

'She was my maths teacher in Year 10 – enthusiastic and positive and always made me feel good about myself. I was in the top group for maths but I never felt confident until she began to teach me ... Unfortunately I changed teacher the next year and my performance went downhill.'

'My geography teacher motivated me so much I thought about being a geography teacher – that is until I had a different A Level teacher.'

'I was not good at sport. Mr X introduced rugby to the school so I was at the same level as everybody else. I played for the school and the Norwich team. He again made me feel I could do it. The other PE teachers would coach the best pupils during lessons leaving the rest of us kick about at the bottom of the field. Without Mr X I would have remained a school-refuser. Why do I remember him? He was kind and was interested in what I could do.'

'I went to a secondary modern school. My headteacher, Mr X, proved that we weren't failures simply because we were not at the grammar school. He fought to enable us to take O Levels and not just CSEs. He timetabled a range of subjects, e.g., army corps, car maintenance, farming, office work as well as pushing the more able pupils to achieve academically. Back in 1967 he encouraged me to take O Level maths in Year 4 (10). He later fought for us to do A Levels at our school.'

'My music teacher changed my life! He spotted my potential straight away. Until then I had been rather average. He encouraged me, made me believe in myself and then there was no stopping me ...'

So, what can we learn from these memories? The one dominant theme which arose from these findings is that adults remember good teachers for their passion and enthusiasm for teaching. Since 1989 in my role as professional development tutor, I have observed hundreds of lessons. There is, however, one lesson I remember above all others. A trainee science teacher was delivering a lesson on electricity that involved explaining to the pupils how to read electric meters. The lesson started brightly enough with the trainee launching the lesson in a reasonably assertive manner. However, as the lesson developed I could see his facial expression, tone of voice and general body language change quite dramatically. The blood drained from the poor fellow's face and it got to the point where he was even failing to make eye contact with the pupils whilst he was explaining the work. You can imagine the impact this had on the behaviour of the pupils in the class – the youngsters began to lose focus and started to chat to each other leaving the poor trainee standing up at the front of the room talking to himself. In our post observation discussion I suggested to him that the root cause of the problem may have been that he simply did not believe that what he was teaching these pupils was the most important thing they were going to learn that day. To his credit he admitted that there was a lot of truth in my comments saying that, when planning the lesson, he had anticipated that the pupils would not be interested in what he had to say. He agreed with me that this belief had led to a self-fulfilling prophesy. He had taught with little conviction and enthusiasm and the pupils had responded accordingly. My response to this was to tell him that teachers should be like actors. Actors do not feel like turning it on all the time, but it is important for them to remember that they have a duty to their audience to perform. The same responsibility applies to the pupil audience in a class. We all have bad days when we really do not feel particularly inspirational, or when we are teaching potentially boring topics. Pupils will forgive this now and again, especially in lessons where we have built up good working relationships. If you are a beginning teacher, you could experience problems with your classes unless you bear this issue in mind. The sign of a good teacher is someone who can fill their pupils with enthusiasm about the most mundane of topics, and convince them that what they are learning is the most important thing since sliced bread.

What absolutely *shouts out* from these findings is the importance of encouragement, and a teacher's belief in the individual. Never underestimate the positive effect of a hand on the shoulder and an encouraging word of praise. As obvious as this advice sounds, I still feel it should be said. I received so many descriptions of teachers who failed to do this and, so, failed to inspire and motivate their pupils.

Organisation, efficiency, classroom control and good pedagogy

Another major criterion of a good teacher that emanated from these responses relates to the issues of classroom management and good pedagogy.

'Very strict, but fair. Insisted that everyone did their best.'

'My geography teacher had excellent class control – she planned the lessons well and made the lessons relevant.'

'The class I was in for biology had in it several boys whose behaviour was not particularly good (our year being the first one to stay on after the fourth year – a gloomy prospect for the local lads who just wanted to leave in January/February and go out to work). With her experience in dealing with "streetwise" city children, Miss X's powers of discipline were superb. She handled these difficult characters with humour and firm approach and her teaching was inspirational to say the least.'

'My English teacher's lessons were perfect. When she entered the room she only had to sit on the desk at the front of the room and the class fell silent – out of respect and anticipation, not out of fear of reprisal.'

'My history teacher was quite a scary and formidable man with such a quiet voice – you had to be quiet to hear what he said.'

'My geography teacher was always fair, always in control – we always knew what the "deal" was.'

'My favourite teachers were firm and assertive – you knew where you were with them and that you would be able to get on in their lessons.'

'My Latin and general studies teacher had an open mind, always made you think, had great debates, never had preconceived ideas but always challenged you to support your views.'

I have long been of the opinion that even the most disruptive of pupils actually want their teachers to take control in the classroom and to challenge them academically. My research and long-standing experience show me that these pupils respect those teachers who manage to do this successfully. Much of this control is down to a teacher's assertive use of body language, eye contact and tone of voice, all of which will be dealt with at a later point in this book.

Using creativity and a sense of humour to make lessons fun

Many examples were given in answer to the questionnaire about teachers being remembered simply because their lessons were fun.

The quotations in the following section are a selective sample of these responses.

'My chemistry teacher, Mr X, was always firm but fair … he would also talk about other things with us. E.g. we had a Polo sucking competition in A Level chemistry.'

'I remember Mr X because he was the stereotypical "mad scientist" type! Very funny and very eccentric. He even looked like "Mr Tefal Man".'

'I remember Mrs X, my biology teacher – she was nice, funny and a good laugh. She was a good teacher.'

'Mr X was very funny, loved his subject, brought it alive and was a bit of an actor. Involved me in a funny production of a play in Spanish in the sixth form. Also told us funny anecdotes about his family life.'

'My favourite teacher at secondary school was Mrs X who taught me English. What I mostly remember was her sarcastic and sharp sense of humour which was quick and intelligent.'

'I remember Mr X for his terrible jokes – he could be strict but you knew where you stood. He encouraged everyone in the class to take part and made it clear that your contributions were valuable. When work was done well you really felt that it was appreciated. The main thing was he made me feel that I could be successful if I was prepared to put the work in. He proved a turning point in my school career and now in my working life, thank you! I can't remember a thing he taught me though, but I do remember the jokes, it's almost as if I still hear them!'

'I remember Mr X who taught me in the last year of primary school. He told us fantastic stories about his life and all the amazing experiences he had. I don't think that half of them were true, but they made good stories. We could tell that he loved us and that he enjoyed teaching us.'

It is not surprising that so many respondents remembered these teachers for their idiosyncratic ways, or sense of fun. You are probably aware that there is a part of the brain called the limbic system. Amongst other functions this part deals with the emotions and long-term memory of the individual. Using humour in the classroom produces a feel-good factor that is retained within the memory for a very long time. Often it is easier to remember a teacher being funny or entertaining, rather than being able to recall the elements of knowledge they taught. That is not to say that this knowledge has not been retained. It is just that it is harder to locate specific incidences when this knowledge was acquired. This view is supported by Professor H. Arsham, Baltimore University, who stated on his website:

> Students appreciate a teacher who gives them something to take home to think about besides homework. One often forgets what one was taught. However, one only can make use of what one has learnt.

What also made teachers so memorable to so many respondents was where teachers used the *personal touch* with their pupils. A small kindness such as having a cup of coffee and an informal chat with a pupil has remained in the long-term memory of one respondent.

Another respondent mentions how, when she was a GCSE pupil, she was sick over a piece of art work and her teacher made her a cup of coffee, gave her some time to compose herself, and then extended her deadline by half a day. Others wrote about how they appreciated the personal touch of their teachers. One respondent recalls how she received a postcard from her language teacher wishing her luck just before her external exams. She went on to say that this is a practice she has now adopted for her pupils.

Although I wanted to be fairly positive in offering role models to you as beginning teachers, I was unable to ignore some of the many responses emanating from the research about bad teachers. Perhaps one of the most telling comments came from a highly respected and highly skilled teacher, and head of year, who made the following observation:

> 'When I was at school I was so appalled by the attitudes of my teachers that I vowed if I ever did end up as a teacher, I would not be like them.'

Some stories were even more negative and bizarre than this. For example, the following story comes from a head of department for English about one of her old English teachers:

> 'I felt very sorry for Mr X who was one of the real eccentrics of teaching. Close to retirement, he often fell asleep in lessons. I remember one lesson vividly when he instructed us to read Chapter X of *Great Expectations*, sat down, fell asleep then woke up before the bell and told us to pack away. We'd kept as quiet as mice so as not to wake him up! He did a lesson on gerunds which I thought was a load of rubbish at the time. Now I know what gerunds are (after twelve years of teaching A Level students) but I still think the lesson was irrelevant!'

'I also remember the names of the rotten teachers and their poor attitudes, lack of fairness, bullying and the distaste they had for pupils –
very sad people.'

'*Real cow* – told me I would never amount to anything! She slapped me
over my hands. I proved her wrong!'

'My form teacher in Year 10 enjoyed inflicting punishment and took
pleasure from his form watching the punishment being inflicted. I tend to
recall those who failed rather than those who succeeded. Mr X (physics)
said there was nobody capable of passing O Level and refused to teach it.
After much pressure, he agreed to let me take the exam, but refused to
teach me – he just gave me the books and told me to get on with it.'

The message that really comes through from this research is that
children have amazingly long memories. Bearing this in mind, we
consequently have to think very carefully about our body language,
our tone of voice and about the way we speak to our young people. I
often tell my beginning teachers that if they treat their Year 7 pupils
with kindness, respect, fairness and firmness, they are likely to have
very few behavioural issues with these youngsters as they move up
through the school. Although the following Chinese proverb puts
these sentiments in a slightly more erudite fashion, the message is still
the same.

A youth is to be regarded with respect. How do you know that his future
will not be equal to our present? (Confucius, Spring and Autumn Period)

We do not always get things right! We should keep in mind that
we are only human after all. If we do get things wrong, then we need
to hold our hands up to our mistakes and make the situation good
with our pupils, since if we fail to do so, then these negative memories
of us as teachers will stay with them for a long time, and possibly
have a detrimental effect as well. In conclusion, read and inwardly
digest this wonderful poem by Gervase Phinn, who sums up the issue
so very well.

Remember Me?

'Do you remember me?' asked the young man.
The old man at the bus stop,
Shabby, standing in the sun, alone,
Looked round.
He stared for a moment, screwing up his eyes,
Then shook his head.
'No, I don't remember you.'
'You used to teach me,' said the young man'
'I've taught so many,' said the old man, sighing,
'I forget.'
'I was the boy you said was useless,
Good for nothing, a waste of space.
Who always left your classroom crying,
And dreaded every lesson that you taught.'
The old man shook his head and turned away.
'No I don't remember you,' he murmured.
'Well, I remember you,' the young man said.

"Remember Me?" from *It Takes One to Know One* (Puffin, London, 2001) is reproduced by kind permission of the author, Gervase Phinn.

How do you want to be remembered?

Chapter 3

What Sort of Teacher are You?

You may recall from reading Chapter 1 that I described the one piece of academic research I hold particularly dear – the work of Zimpher and Howey. In their 1987 paper, they wrote at length about what they call the 'personal domain' of a teacher. It is this domain that forms the specific focus of this chapter. Here, the conception of teaching is one of a 'self-actualised person' who uses him or herself as an effective and humane instrument of classroom instruction. The term 'self-actualised' implies strongly that a teacher possesses a high level of self-knowledge. You might be forgiven for asking how the acquisition of self-knowledge can help teachers to establish, maintain and develop good relationships with their pupils. My response is simple. Competence in this domain requires teachers to develop and hone fully their intra-personal skills. They can do this both by raising their level of self-awareness and by being critical in analysis of relationships with other people. Therefore, teachers need full competence in this domain to understand fully the interactional nature of teaching. With full knowledge of their strengths, weaknesses and emotional needs teachers are able to make informed decisions about the ways in which they deal with their pupils. This then allows them to provide a warm and supportive learning environment. The aim of this chapter is, therefore, to make possible scenarios whereby you, as beginning teachers, will be able to ask questions of yourselves, and where you can explore the impact of your teaching style on the relationships with your pupils.

One of the first issues to focus on is that of the self-esteem of teachers. Simply put, teachers with high esteem produce pupils with high esteem. Unfortunately, however, the converse is also true. It is fair to say that people with low self-esteem do not value their personal qualities, nor do they see themselves as being very capable. Often this view is contrary to the way others see them.

I have found in my experience that teachers with low self-esteem tend to be defensive, extremely sensitive to criticism and rather intolerant of alternative viewpoints. Very often they see an attempt to get them to practise reflectivity as a personal slight on their teaching capabilities. So, how do these behaviours impact on their relationships with pupils? Put quite simply, these teachers struggle to establish and maintain meaningful learning relationships with their pupils. What these teachers tend to do is to *personalise* inappropriate behaviour by pupils, viewing their behaviour as a personal attack on them, rather than as a manifestation of any inner difficulties the pupil concerned may be experiencing. A teacher with low self-esteem often finds it very difficult to distance him or herself from the pupil's poor behaviour. In other words, they see everything that happens in the classroom as being about *them* and not about the pupils. A particular example that comes to mind is where a young teacher overheard one of his pupils saying that he 'hated' him. This newly qualified teacher, who had only been teaching for about a term, understandably became quite upset about this remark, reacted angrily, and took the incident as a personal affront to his professionalism. My role was to try to get him to take a step back from the incident and view this inappropriate behaviour from the pupil's perspective. I tried to get him to see that there is usually a rationale and a history behind the inappropriate actions of pupils. I told this teacher that, if there was this negative feeling towards him, then it was important to find out why this was the case and then to try to tackle the issues that were bothering this youngster, to adopt an *inquisitorial* rather than *adversarial* stance and to discuss the issue with the pupil involved. I asked this newly qualified teacher to think carefully about the body language he used when talking to this youngster, and to remember that a discussion involves *listening* as well as speaking. He did this and very soon came back to me in a very different frame of mind. It turned out that the youngster had been annoyed and hurt because he felt he had been humiliated in front of the class for not doing his homework properly, and for being made to do the work again. Both the teacher and the boy learned something from this incident. The teacher learned that using sarcasm and ridicule to belittle pupils in class, in order to score points, was unacceptable and counter-productive. He also began to understand that this incident had occurred primarily because of his high level of uncertainty and his low self-esteem in this particular situation. He was fairly new to this class and was worried about the lack of home-work coming in from pupils and had taken this as a personal slight to himself. As the discussion unfurled, the pupil had begun to see things from the teacher's perspective, and learned some alternative ways of dealing with issues such as these. I can assure you that these types of situations do not just happen to inexperienced teachers. In one of my classes, for example, I suddenly began to feel a degree of antipathy towards me from one of my Year 10 pupils with whom, up to this point, I had got on with quite well. Let us call her Kate. There was nothing overtly aggressive about her behaviour, but I just had a gut feeling that things were not quite right. Having looked at her prior attainment data, I knew that she was seriously underachieving, so I decided to tackle her about this one evening after school. Kate was initially quite defensive and did not really want to talk about the issue. At this point I had to reassure her that however personal her remarks might be, and whatever she had to say, I would try not to take offence. I added that I just needed to know what was going on. By using a non-confrontational tone of voice and sympathetic body language, I found out the root cause of the issue. It turned out that her sister and my daughter had fallen out and that she felt, because of this, I did not like her. I was absolutely amazed at this disclosure but fortunately I managed to dispel these preconceptions, and things soon returned to normal. I need to make two points about this incident; had I not had the confidence to try to ascertain the history and rationale behind Kate's behaviour, things would simply have festered and our relationship would have broken down completely. In my early years of teaching, I would not have been secure enough nor would I have had the self-esteem to open up such a can of worms. Over the course of my teaching career I have trained myself to deal with situations such as these with, hopefully, a reasonable degree of success.

Having tutored dozens of beginning teachers I realise that the development of self-esteem is not necessarily an exponential process. If self-esteem could be displayed in the form of a graph, it would not be shown as a smooth continuum. It is more likely that the graph would show a series of peaks and troughs showing both periods of real self-belief and confidence, and periods of great self-doubt and depression. Hopefully, however, one would expect an overall rise in teacher confidence and self-esteem to correlate with increasing levels of experience. It is not within the remit of this book to explore the general psychological reasons behind a teacher's lack of esteem, so I have, therefore, limited my discussion to those factors affected by a teacher's experience in schools. The acquisition of high self-esteem depends on a number of things: the personality of the teacher; the experiences of the teacher within their school; the level of formal and informal support the teacher receives from his or her colleagues. It would also be highly hypocritical of me to say that well-established and successful members of staff do not experience self-doubts and periods of low self-esteem. Of course they do, but the more secure teachers learn from their experiences and manage to get to grips with these feelings sooner rather than later, and then simply manage to get on with the job. Very often it is through dealing with specific incidents reflectively that we learn how to increase our self-esteem. So what advice would I offer beginning teachers on how to deal with potentially difficult incidents, whilst at the same time developing and maintaining one's self-esteem?

- Be aware that you could be making the issues personal and try to step back from the incident and view the situation with the needs of the pupil in mind.
- Try to avoid *external* pressures whilst dealing with the pupil, or with specific incidents. For example, try not to worry too much about how some of your more robust colleagues may view the way you deal with issues such as these.
- Try to get *behind* the words and the body language of the pupil you are dealing with. Ascertain what these verbal and non-verbal signals are saying about the person sending the message. Find out their needs from the conversation.
- Once you have discovered the needs of the pupil, try to respond appropriately. This may be something you can deal with immediately, it may need a degree of planning or, alternatively, require you to gain the assistance of another, more experienced professional. Accepting that you cannot always

deal with some issues on your own is an important learning point.

- Ensure that the pupil knows that you will always be there for him or her. Do not close off all the lines of communication. Remember that some pupils prefer to write things down, so you may have to give them the opportunity to do this. However, be very careful about the issue of disclosure. You must inform the youngster that you may have to pass on sensitive information to the head of year.

- Make sure you hold on to your self-esteem. The specific issue should be about the pupil, and not you.

- Above all, make sure that you learn from the experience. If you have followed the advice offered above, you will have dealt with the incident more successfully than if you had simply gone in with all guns blazing. Take heart from this; congratulate yourself; make a conscious effort to elevate your self-esteem; accept where things did not go quite according to plan; mentally reflect on what you could have done differently; accept that any mistakes made are simply opportunities for learning. By doing this you will remain in control of the process – it is this control that will help to reinforce your self-esteem.

Humphreys (1995) described how teachers with low to middle self-esteem tend to project themselves when dealing with pupils in their charge. The teacher puts the responsibility for their lives onto their pupils. For example, if I say, 'you're really getting me down', I am giving you a lot of power over me and am relinquishing my own responsibility for my own needs. Let us be honest here, we have all had classes where individual pupils have really got to us; where they have evoked strong feelings of impotence; where they have done their best to undermine our authority; where they seem to be able to set the agenda for the lesson. In other words, when these youngsters are absent from the class, we are different and more confident teachers. It is difficult for any teacher to deal with pupils like this, let alone a beginning teacher. Much of the issue lies with the self-esteem of the teacher. Although probably unable to articulate this, the pupil has managed to seek out the vulnerabilities and low self-esteem of the teacher, and has then gone in for the kill. This type of pupil can evoke two extreme reactions from teachers with low self-esteem. They are either allowed to have the run of the classroom and do just what they want, or they become the subject of a personal battle between them and their teacher. None of these scenarios are beneficial to the teacher, or to the pupil. Sometimes, merely understanding the issue can often help a teacher to adopt a more balanced perspective towards the problem and allow them to deal with the pupil in a more objective and distanced manner. By employing this approach, the inappropriate behaviour of the pupil is being focused on and not the character traits of the individual. I have often found that by stepping back and using the methods prescribed above to deal with individual pupils such as these, I have obtained a different perspective from the one expected, and harmony has, once again, been restored.

So how does all of this marry in with the main theme of the book – that is, how to both establish, maintain and develop good working relationships with pupils? Quite simply, the more skilled a teacher becomes in raising their own self-esteem, the more they will be able to deal positively with the pupils within their charge. It is a mistake, therefore, to think that the only people who need developing are the pupils. Teaching is an interactive process – both parties need to learn and to grow.

In order to help beginning teachers to do just this, I have provided a set of descriptions of teacher/pupil relationships, which were based on the excellent work of Humphreys (1995) who identified six types of teacher/pupil relationship. These descriptions can be seen in Figure 3.1. Alongside each description I have included a list of questions for you to think about.

As helpful as the descriptions may be, it needs to be said that the placing of these teacher behaviours into categories is somewhat problematic. I challenge any teacher, experienced or otherwise, to say that their teaching behaviour fits neatly into any of the descriptions. In my opinion, we can all identify elements of our teaching, at some point in our careers, from each one of these categories. I would even go so far as to say that during a typical academic year, even the most talented and gifted teachers amongst us fail to realise the criteria described in the final category, more than 80 per cent of the time. We are all human, have times when we are not at our best, and we cannot be expected to reach this high standard day after day. What is important, however, is that we should be fully aware of the impact that our

Characteristics (Low teacher self-esteem)	Questions to ask yourself
Absence of relationship In this classroom the teacher tends to teach the class as a whole and fails to make any real meaningful relationships with any of the pupils. The question that must arise here is what are they doing in teaching?	**Is this you?** Do you recognise any of these characteristics in your teaching? Are there any pupils in your classes with whom you do not have a good working relationship? What have you done about it? Do you recognise these characteristics in other teachers you know? How do you feel about these teachers?
Relationship devoid of feeling It is recognised that this teacher is a good technician in as much as they prepare their lessons well and provide the necessary material required for academic success. They are good disciplinarians and experience very few problems in the classroom. However, the teacher shows little obvious warmth and/or closeness to pupils. The teacher is simply there to teach.	**Is this you?** Do you recognise any of these characteristics? Do you focus too much on the technical side of teaching? (technical domain) Do you need to develop the personal domain? Do you need to give more attention to how you teach rather than what you teach? Do you understand the full role of the teacher? How aware are you of the different types of intelligence? Do you cater for these in your lesson planning? What satisfaction do you get out of teaching? Do you recognise these characteristics in other teachers you know? What do you think of these teachers?
Narcissistic relationship This type of teacher does establish relationships with their pupils but these are very much conditional. When the pupils meet the teacher's needs they gain approval. Failure to meet their demands will lead to a breakdown of relationships and negativity from the teacher. In this relationship the standard of pupils' behaviour becomes the key method of measuring their worth.	**Is this you?** Are your relationships with pupils conditional? Do you recognise any of these characteristics? Do you enjoy good working relationships with pupils who don't think like you? Do you have pro-school and anti-school sub-cultures within your classes? What do you do about this? Does your lesson planning cater for the interests of all pupils in your classes? Do you recognise these characteristics in other teachers you know? What do you think of these teachers?

Figure 3.1: Six types of teacher/pupil relationship (continued)

Characteristics (Low teacher self-esteem)	Questions to ask yourself

Over-involved relationships

This type of teacher really needs to be needed and will go to extremes in order to be needed by their pupils. This teacher feels they are indispensable and will work extra long hours and/or take on far more than they should in order to develop this indispensability. Very often this is all done at a sub-conscious level but the strong message to their pupils is that, as long as you value me for what I do for you, I will accept and approve of you. Pupils who reject these conditions and who prefer to be independent decision-makers, are likely to be rejected by this teacher.

Is this you?

Do you recognise any of these characteristics in your teaching?

Do you try to interfere in the personal lives of your pupils?

Do you hold on to information that really needs to be shared?

Do you take on responsibility at school in order to be needed?

Do you take time off work when you need to?

Are you able to delegate?

Do you overtly seek approval from your pupils?

Do you fish for compliments from your pupils?

Do you enjoy good relationships with pupils who don't appear to need you?

Do you enjoy good relationships with pupils who don't think like you?

Do you recognise these characteristics in other teachers you know?

What do you think of these teachers?

Symbiotic relationships

In this teacher's class there is very little room for individuality. The teacher holds a corporate view of the class whereby the pupils' needs are subjugated to serve the *whole*. Interdependence rather than independence is highly valued. In this situation, each pupil requires the approval of both teacher and other pupils to feel valued. As a result of this, pupil self-esteem is low.

Is this you?

Do you recognise any of these characteristics in your teaching?

Do you use the corporate power of the class to impose disapproval on sanction breakers?

Do you show respect and approval for those pupils who break the mould?

Do you enjoy good working relationships with pupils who don't think like you?

Do you recognise these characteristics in other teachers you know?

What do you think of these teachers?

Figure 3.1: Six types of teacher/pupil relationship (continued)

Characteristics (High teacher self-esteem)	Questions to ask yourself
Empathic relationship The teacher enjoys a healthy relationship with pupils. Relationships are of an unconditional nature where each pupil is valued for him or herself irrespective of their social background, academic ability and attitude towards school. This teacher shows an interest in pupils because they value and respect them for their uniqueness as human beings. This type of teacher is known as an 'affirming teacher' because he or she values the relationship with the pupil above all else. No amount of inappropriate behaviour, mistakes or failures will break that relationship. This teacher, however, is not a soft touch. The teacher holds strong views about what constitutes acceptable and non-acceptable behaviour but any sanctions imposed are carried out within a framework of a warm affirming relationship. The teacher takes every opportunity to help the pupil learn to take responsibility for his or her own actions. The teacher does not overtly criticise or put down pupils nor do they use sarcasm to try to change their behaviour. This teacher values the pupils by giving them a chance to make a constructive contribution to any sanctions imposed.	**Is this you?** Do you recognise any of these characteristics in your teaching? Do you value all the pupils in your classes or do you let some slip through the net? How important is the delivery of subject knowledge in your lessons? Is the pupil/teacher relationship the most important facet of your teaching? How do you show your pupils that you understand their uniqueness as individuals? Do you impose your sanctions within a warm caring and affirming framework? Do you give your pupils an opportunity to make a constructive contribution to disciplinary procedures? Do you recognise these characteristics in other teachers you know? What do you think of these teachers?

Figure 3.1: Six types of teacher/pupil relationship (continued)

behaviours can have on our pupils, and for us to try hard not to behave towards our youngsters in a damaging and inappropriate way. However, this should not be seen as a one-way process! Your pupils too have a large part to play here. They have to realise that people in the adult world, represented in school by teachers, are different from each other. An invaluable part of the hidden curriculum is the pupils' gradual realisation that they have to make many adjustments to the varying demands of teachers in school. It is part of their preparation for adult life and, as such, is as important as mathematics, English and science. They learn that there are some teachers they like and others they cannot stand the sight of; that some teachers appear to like them and that others do not.

Styles of management and teaching

One of the things you as beginning teachers have to decide on early in your teaching careers is the management and teaching style you are going to employ in the classroom. Your choice of style determines the climate of your classroom and, ultimately, the quality of your relationships with your pupils. I have adapted the work of Lewin *et al.* (1939; cited in Rogers, 1998), to draw up a continuum of possible teaching styles to support the text below. This is shown in Figure 3.2 on the following page. Read through the text and try to ascertain where you currently fit along this continuum.

Following Figure 3.2, I have put together composite portraits of a typical lesson taught by an indecisive, an autocratic and a democratic teacher to highlight the different teaching styles.

Lewin *et al.* used the term *'laissez-faire'* to describe a teaching style not supported by known rules and routines, and firm expectations and sanctions, and where pretty much anything goes. As useful as this contribution is, I am not totally happy with this description, because I feel that there are many teachers who do have good intentions, who do outline their expectations and who do employ sanctions, but who fail to do this consistently. In my opinion, it is this very inconsistency and indecisiveness that undermines good teacher/pupil relationships. Pupils simply do not know where they stand. For the purposes of this book, therefore, I will refer to these types of teachers as 'indecisive' teachers.

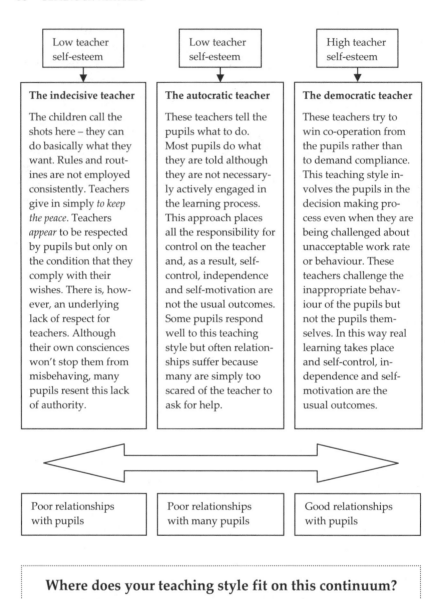

Low teacher self-esteem	Low teacher self-esteem	High teacher self-esteem
The indecisive teacher	**The autocratic teacher**	**The democratic teacher**
The children call the shots here – they can do basically what they want. Rules and routines are not employed consistently. Teachers give in simply *to keep the peace*. Teachers *appear* to be respected by pupils but only on the condition that they comply with their wishes. There is, however, an underlying lack of respect for teachers. Although their own consciences won't stop them from misbehaving, many pupils resent this lack of authority.	These teachers tell the pupils what to do. Most pupils do what they are told although they are not necessarily actively engaged in the learning process. This approach places all the responsibility for control on the teacher and, as a result, self-control, independence and self-motivation are not the usual outcomes. Some pupils respond well to this teaching style but often relationships suffer because many are simply too scared of the teacher to ask for help.	These teachers try to win co-operation from the pupils rather than to demand compliance. This teaching style involves the pupils in the decision making process even when they are being challenged about unacceptable work rate or behaviour. These teachers challenge the inappropriate behaviour of the pupils but not the pupils themselves. In this way real learning takes place and self-control, independence and self-motivation are the usual outcomes.
Poor relationships with pupils	Poor relationships with many pupils	Good relationships with pupils

Where does your teaching style fit on this continuum?

Figure 3.2:   Continuum of teaching and management styles

The indecisive teacher

Teacher X is a nice man who wants to be liked and who really wants to succeed as a mathematics teacher. He has planned the content of his lesson reasonably well, but knows from the start that things are not going to go according to plan. He is expecting trouble from a group of boys in his Year 9 class but, although he has been given plenty of advice from colleagues, he has not arrived at the lesson with any definite strategies for dealing with any potential disruption.

Year 9 enter the room very noisily. 'That's OK, they will settle down soon', thinks Mr X who puts his head down and busies himself by flicking through some papers on his desk. The pupils do not settle down. Mr X is now getting a little worried about the noise level in the room. It is an old classroom with high ceilings and he is concerned that his colleagues in the adjacent rooms will hear this noise. What will they think of him? 'Sshssh', he says in a pleading voice 'will you please keep quiet now? Please settle down.' The noise continues. In desperation, he pleads 'If you keep making that noise you won't be able to play the game I've got planned for you.' Eventually, after a great deal of effort, Mr X feels he is ready to move on. 'Quiet, please, whilst I take the register,' says Mr X who has his pen in his hand and his head down looking at his mark book. Most of the pupils eventually comply with his request but, yes, you've guessed it, the 'Mafia' in the back row are having none of it. They carry on talking regardless. Mr X takes the register even though many of the pupils are still chatting to each other and generally larking about.

'Right, this is what we are going to do today,' says Mr X cheer-fully. 'First, I am going to check that you understood the equations we did yesterday, and then we are going to do some more book work. If you are good then we will play a mathematical game for the last fifteen minutes of the lesson.'

Instead of Mr X *asking* the pupils how to do the equations, he *tells* the pupils how these are done whilst writing some examples on the board. As soon as he turns away from the class, the boys on the back row start talking loudly and hitting each other. 'Quiet boys, please' shouts Mr X getting more and more exasperated. 'It's not fair on the others – if you don't behave yourself the class won't get their game.' 'It's not our fault,' Gary says. 'We don't understand the work. You never help us!' he shouts. 'Why do you have to be so rude, Gary? Would you talk to your mother like that?' 'Yes, I would,' Gary yells out laughingly, looking around for an audience to share the joke with. 'Well, the reason you don't understand this work is simply because you weren't listening when I was explaining things to you', said Mr X. 'You were messing about at the back.' 'No we weren't, we couldn't hear you – you were turning away from us. It's not our fault. You always pick on us. You can ask anyone. Ask Dawn – she'll tell you!' 'He's right sir, you do pick on them,' piped up Dawn. 'Leave him alone, he's only trying to do his job,' yells out Teresa who is getting fed up with the whole business. 'Just be quiet both of you and let me explain the work,' shouts Mr X who is getting increasingly hot under the collar. '*Bloody hell*, I'm only trying to help you', shouts Teresa aggressively. 'I won't bother in future.' 'Please don't use language like that Teresa. You should know better. Your mum didn't bring you up like that.' 'You don't know anything about my family!' snarls Teresa. Fifteen minutes has passed, the lesson has degenerated into chaos and no learning has yet taken place. The same pattern continues for the rest of the lesson – but, in order to keep the peace, Mr X allows the pupils to have their game that lasts half an hour, and not the fifteen minutes promised at the beginning of the lesson. In order to make amends for the way the lesson has gone, he makes Dawn, Gary and Teresa team captains for the game.

Mr X left the classroom exhausted and demoralised. He had fail-ed, because he was unable to realise his lesson objectives and because he had got angry with the class. Needless to say the group of boys at the back enjoyed the lesson immensely.

The question we have to ask ourselves is why Mr X's indecisive teaching style was so ineffective. I have outlined the reasons below.

- He did not come to the lesson with any behaviour management strategies in mind. He knew that there were going to be problems, but felt it was beyond his capabilities to prevent these.
- Since his tone of voice and body language were not assertive enough, he showed indecision and prevarication.
- He did not dominate the teaching space sufficiently enough to be listened to by his pupils.
- He became entwined in pupils' secondary behaviour – the arguments with Gary, Dawn and Teresa got out of hand simply because he did not cut the discussion short.
- He simply failed to impose his will on the pupils.
- He left it too late to show his displeasure and, as a result, was left with very little option but to shout at the class.
- Despite all his good intentions, he allowed the pupils to set the agenda for the lesson. Not only did they get their game even though they had behaved inappropriately, but Mr X extended the time allocation for this by fifteen minutes, simply to *keep the peace* and to calm things down. He rewarded the bad behaviour of the three miscreants by appointing them as team captains.
- He hoped for compliance, believing that his friendliness and reasonableness would win the pupils round, but this simply did not happen. He also hoped that his goodwill gesture of extending the game would make the pupils like him and that, consequently, they would do the work set by him. This did not happen either.

> **Do you recognise any of your teaching behaviours here?**
> (Chapters 5 and 6 will help you to address some of these issues)

The autocratic teacher

There are certain teachers in most schools with whom pupils simply do not mess. If they have a bad day, then everybody knows it.

Mr Y enters the room. By the time he has walked to the front of the classroom, most of the pupils are quiet and ready to listen attentively. However, there are a couple of pupils chancing their arms at the back of the room by finishing off their conversation. Mr Y could have ignored this but chose not to. 'Hey, you two!' shouts Mr Y staring fiercely at the two youngsters. 'How dare you talk when I come into the room! You two are always talking when you shouldn't be. How many times do I have to tell you about this! Don't do that again! Understand!' 'Yes' the two pupils say rather sulkily. 'Yes, sir!' shouts Mr Y. 'Yes, sir,' they comply.

Mr Y starts the lesson but is interrupted by the two at the back smiling at each other. This is not a good move. It is time for a showdown. 'Who do you two think you are?' he yells. He thinks, this is my lesson and no one does that to me. 'Do that again and I'll come down on you like a ton of bricks!' The rest of the pupils start to fidget uncomfortably and look nervously at Mr Y. He moves the pupils away from each other to disparate parts of the room.

Mr Y explains the work once, and then circulates the classroom checking that pupils are working. When he gets to the miscreants, he stands behind them in an attempt to intimidate them, to show them who is the boss. When he has made his point, he returns to the front of the room where he sits down for most of the remainder of the lesson. If he hears someone talking, even quietly, he makes a sarcastic and caustic comment designed to embarrass those concerned.

Mr Y is also not averse to using insults to put his pupils down. 'Are you thick, boy?' He yells at a pupil who tells him he does not

understand the work and has been asking his neighbour for advice. As he looks up he notices that Michael has got black trainers on. 'What are those things you've got on your feet?' he yells at Michael fiercely. 'They're trainers sir, but they're black just like shoes. I've got my old shoes in my locker but they're falling apart. My mum says she'll get some shoes for Monday when she gets her benefits, but that I'm to wear these for the time being.' 'Go and change those now, Michael.' 'But sir, I can't wear my old shoes, they're falling apart.' 'I don't care, go and change them or else you'll have me to answer to.' 'I'm not changing them sir. I have explained why I can't put my shoes on. They're falling apart! I've told you sir!' Mr Y begins to realise that someone has to back down here but it's not going to be him. 'Go to your head of year,' he yells slamming a textbook down on the desk. 'If you are in my classroom you obey my rules! If you don't like my rules you can stand outside the classroom for the rest of the lesson. It makes no difference to me!'

On the face of it, Mr Y appears to be an effective teacher. He does not get much trouble from pupils – his reputation sees to that. Mr Y is proud of his standing within the school. If you passed his room, all the pupils would appear to be working and, above all, to be behaving themselves. It would also be quite understandable for a beginning teacher who, believing that a quiet classroom is a learning classroom, would want to aspire to establish a similar disciplinary hold over their pupils. The question you need to ask, however, is whether this is an effective classroom environment for real learning to take place. The teacher/pupil relationship in this classroom is one of fear and not respect. Mr Y does not respect his pupils and the pupils most certainly do not respect Mr Y. The dominant climate in this classroom is adversarial, with Mr Y feeling that the pupils should obey him at all times and that he should win every discipline battle he encounters during the course of his normal teaching day. Mr Y is a teacher with low self-esteem who is frightened to let things go, even a little. He is worried that if he relinquishes his control over the pupils then chaos will reign and he will be left alone with his vulnerabilities.

There is nothing wrong in a teacher being demanding. Nor is there any issue about a teacher being authoritative when they need to be. That is all part of the job. However, an authoritarian and autocratic teacher such as Mr Y, does the profession a great disservice. The overbearing, sarcastic and aggressive attitude which he displays towards his pupils has the effect of stripping them of their self-esteem, dignity and rights as human beings. There is no way that real learning can take place in a scenario such as this. Autocratic teachers like Mr Y:

- do not like children;
- demand compliance from their pupils;
- see the classroom as a war zone, with them as the eventual victors;
- give orders to pupils, instead of requests;
- remove the opportunities for pupils to make choices;
- verbally threaten the pupils regularly;
- nag at, and preach to pupils;
- use sarcasm, humiliation, verbal aggression to control;
- rarely smile or share a joke;
- laugh *at* pupils but not *with* them;
- make inappropriate personal remarks about the pupils;
- engender fear, not respect.

I suspect that, in the past, autocratic teachers like Mr Y would probably have resorted to physical sanctions to support their discipline. This could have been done through the formal use of the school's corporal punishment system, or more likely through some form of physical assault on the pupils. Tempting as it may be at times, you are strongly advised to keep your hands off your pupils. In a world of increasing litigation you would do well to heed the advice offered in this extract from the guideline document produced by the National Union of Teachers (2000).

> The physical restraint of a particular pupil, or pupils, should not be considered a regular or routine act. The use of physical restraint of pupils on a regular basis will place the teacher at both physical and professional risk. Teachers should not feel obliged to intervene where their own personal safety is at risk or where intervention could lead to accusations of either assault or child abuse.

Do you recognise any of your teaching behaviours here?
(Chapters 5 and 6 will help you to address some of these issues)

The democratic teacher

The democratic teacher is the successful teacher. You should aspire to this teaching style if you want to develop good learning relationships with your pupils. Although many teachers develop this teaching style as they become more experienced, you do not necessarily have to be *old* to be a decisive or democratic teacher. I come across many teachers who display many of those qualities which are needed to be a democratic teacher, either in their induction year, or certainly within a few years in teaching. Conversely, I have also encountered a lot of older and *so-called* more experienced teachers, whose teaching style is far from democratic, and who are unlikely ever to be able to adopt this approach with their pupils. It is, therefore, all about having the right *attitude*, and showing a willingness to reflect positively on your teaching and interactions with your pupils. Miss Z, a young geography teacher who has been teaching in the same school for the past four years, is one such teacher. She would, however, be the first to admit that earlier on in her career, she had made a number of basic mistakes. When looking back over her brief teaching career, she realised that she simply had not been authoritative enough with her pupils during her first two years at the school. She would also accept that, in those early days, much of her teaching behaviour matched the description of the typically indecisive teacher given to you earlier in this chapter. Things are very different now. So what happened that she was able to turn things around so dramatically? Despite being told repeatedly about the importance of establishing rules and routines in her classroom, about the importance of being objective and consistent when dealing with disciplinary issues, she really only took this on board towards the end of her second year. Her way simply was not working and she began to realise that things had to change. It seems that it took almost two years for Miss Z to assimilate all the advice and guidance given to her and to understand the rationale behind the school's induction programme. She is now well on the way to becoming a decisive and democratic teacher and a well-respected member of staff. So what exactly are the characteristics of a democratic teacher? The following description will give you a flavour of the classroom atmosphere engendered by such a teacher.

Miss Z had developed clear rules and routines for this Year 9 class at the beginning of the year. Up to now, this has paid dividends as far as pupil behaviour is concerned. However, she now senses that the honeymoon period is over, and that some of the pupils are beginning to misbehave and to try their luck in her lessons.

Miss Z stands in the middle of the room, adopts a positive and confident body posture and scans the class who are now expecting her to speak. 'Right 9M, put your equipment down and look this way. I said, look this way! I want to make eye contact with every single one of you.' After about thirty seconds, and a lot of scanning by Miss Z, the pupils all comply with her instructions.

'I have been extremely pleased with the way you have all settled into this class. Your work has been of a good standard and, generally speaking, you have all shown a pretty good attitude towards learning, and towards the rules and routines we agreed on at the beginning of the year. You may remember that we discussed the reasons why we have these rules; to allow everybody to reach their potential in a comfortable and pleasant learning environment. However, I have become a little concerned recently that some of you are going off the boil, in terms of your behaviour and attitudes to your work. I feel, therefore, that it is now time for us to re-visit those rules, routines and expectations. We're going to do this as a quiz and there will be a small prize of a chocolate bar for the top two pupils. After this, we will get on with the main thrust of the lesson, that is, to explore the effects of locating a superstore near an already congested area of the town. So, will you please get your books out and we can make a start. Thank you.'

Miss Z is happy to use up the twenty minutes or so it will take to reinforce her expectations. She knows that making this investment now will save her a lot of time and effort chasing up on inevitable discipline or work-related problems at a later date. She was so sure about doing this, that she wrote this activity into her lesson plan. The quiz goes well and, having dispensed the chocolate bars, Miss Z is ready to launch the lesson.

Miss Z simply stands at the front of the class, scanning the pupils and making calming signals with her hands. The majority of pupils become quiet. The remainder of the pupils fall into line on her verbal cue; 'Right, we are ready to start now – everything down, eyes forward and give me your full attention, please.' This does the trick and very soon all pupils become attentive. Rather than launching straight into the lesson objectives, Miss Z asks the following question: 'Who lives near to a superstore, or who has visited anyone living near to a superstore?' Knowing that there is a superstore within the catchment area, she is on fairly safe ground when using this question to launch the topic. Virtually all of the hands go up in response. Miss Z also puts her hand up. (This is a deliberate ploy on her part to create a sense of corporate identity within the class.) At this point, Miss Z thanks the pupils for their answers and then asks them to focus their attention on the lesson objectives that have already been written on the whiteboard. Having read these objectives out to the class, she then asks the pupils to copy them down into their books. 'We have now seen that many of us live fairly close to a superstore. Now I want you to tell me what's good, and what's bad about living near a superstore. I want to see if you can come up with at least four good things and four bad things. Remember that it is important for you to remember to put your hands up if you want to make a contribution. Jessica and Graham, will you come up to the board to record the responses?' Again, virtually all of the pupils put their hands up. Miss Z repeats or paraphrases the pupils' responses, and Jessica and Graham write these down on the board. In their sheer enthusiasm to be heard, a number of pupils shout their answers out. Miss Z, aware that she needs to stamp this out, stops the class, scans the room and pauses dramatically before saying: 'Well done to all those pupils who want to make a responses, but I need to remind you about our rule for getting heard in this classroom. You must put your hand up if you want to answer a question. Most of you are doing this, but I would like *all* of you to obey this rule. Thank you.' The situation improves dramatically, but there are still a few pupils who continue to call out their answers. Miss Z, wanting to continue the flow of the lesson, tactically ignores this for a while, and then frowns at the miscreants and puts her fingers to her lips – this seems to do the trick. These pupils immediately put their hands up. Things are not going perfectly by any means. Aaron is chewing, Roger and Alan are looking out of the window and Sharon is swinging back on her chair. Miss Z clicks her fingers to gain their attention. She then points her index finger to one of her eyes in order to convey her demand that the two boys look at her, and she then follows this up with the *stare*. To stop Sharon swinging on her chair, all Miss Z does is to make eye contact with her, and use her hand to draw Sharon towards her. This only leaves Aaron to deal with. She knows Aaron well – she knows that he loves an audience, and would absolutely relish having to make the journey up to the front of the room. So, rather than ask him to come out to the front of the class to put his gum in the bin, she adopts a different tactic. She takes the bin over to him, gives him a brief smile and looks at him expectantly until he eventually puts his gum in the bin. She then turns away and carries on with the lesson. Because the signals have all been learned before, all four pupils are in no doubt as to what is expected of them, and they comply with a minimum of fuss. No one has lost face, discipline has been maintained and, very importantly, the flow of the lesson has not been disrupted.

So, why does this approach work? Miss Z has learned over the past three years to develop an authoritative approach towards her teaching. Rogers (1998) and Dixie (2003) described the way the use of such an approach could produce an effective classroom management scenario, and help to build meaningful relationships with pupils. Miss Z does a number of things right; she uses an assertive tone of voice; she chooses her words carefully when giving directives to pupils, and she makes optimum use of eye contact; she adopts a confident and positive body posture. By doing this, she produces an expectation within her pupils that they will accept her authority. Kyriacou, (2001: 103) made the point superbly when he wrote:

> If teachers behave as though they have authority, it is surprising how far this attitude exerts a momentum of its own, leading pupils to behave accordingly ...

What, then, is the difference between an authoritative and an authoritarian teacher?

Authoritarian teachers do not always read the signals correctly – that is why they often experience conflict with the more strong-willed pupils in their classes. They see the classroom as an arena in which to do battle and where they must win at all costs. They do not understand the need to withdraw tactically at certain times, and/or with certain pupils. There is nothing more embarrassing than having to witness a major row between a fellow colleague and an angry pupil, especially when you feel that the youngster has been pushed into a corner, and where you hold a degree of sympathy for their predicament. Authoritative and democratic teachers really know their pupils. They are able to see immediately whether a youngster is having a bad day and, although certainly not sanctioning inappropriate behaviour, they are prepared to wait until a later time to deal with it. A confident teacher with high self-esteem will do this. I remember attending a lecture by the education consultant, Bill Rogers, where he talked about the use of sanctions – he used the term 'certainty, not severity'. This advice has stuck in my mind and is something I have tried to incorporate in my teaching, and to pass on to the beginning teachers in my school. It is important for you to understand that things do not have to be dealt with there and then. When a pupil is really wound up and ready to have a go, it is often advisable to leave things well alone until the pupil has calmed down. If you are worried about losing face, try to step back and to remember that the inappropriate behaviour of this pupil is not a personal slight on you. When you are in the heat of the moment, however, this is not an easy thing to do. I remember one incident in my first year of secondary school teaching in an extremely challenging school in West London. I had had a run-in with one particular boy whose behaviour during my lesson had been totally unacceptable. Let us call him Gary. Quite honestly, I should have kept Gary behind at break and sorted things out quietly and calmly, but because I felt that his misbehaviour was very much a personal attack on me, I did not want to talk to the boy. However, I very soon paid for my mistake. I was just about to launch a geography lesson with my Year 10 class, when Gary burst into the room, knocked over a few chairs and started swearing and insulting me. You can imagine that, as a young and inexperienced teacher, I was quite taken aback. In fact, although I tried to appear outwardly calm, I was inwardly shaking.

Gary then stormed out of the room. He was excluded for a period of two weeks. I learned two lessons from this experience. The first was that I could have prevented the whole incident from occurring in the first place, by dealing with the earlier incident in a more objective and less personalised manner. My personal pride, however, had stood in the way of me doing this. My second learning experience occurred three years later once Gary had left school. He took the trouble to come back to see me to tell me how he was getting on. He apologised to me for his outburst and explained to me that his mum and dad had split up the evening before the incident, and that he was angry and simply 'looking for a fight'. I was the first person he had come across. I must say that I felt very humbled by his apology. 'There is no need for you to apologise to me, Gary,' I told him. 'I was the adult and I should have read the situation better. Please accept *my* apologies.' We parted on very good terms.

You will remember Mr X, the autocratic teacher. He constantly nagged, bullied and preached to his pupils. Authoritative teachers, such as Miss Z, do not nag or preach. They know that is the worst thing that they can do! Teenagers simply hate nags! You have only got to look at the rolling eyes, and the negative body language of a pupil who is being given a right good scolding by the school nag, to see the effect it can have on teacher/pupil relationships, and subsequently on their learning. In general, authoritative teachers keep calm, refer to previously launched rules and, in order to create maximum impact, keep their admonitions to an absolute minimum. They do not make personal attacks on the pupils, preferring instead to make the unacceptable nature of the pupil's behaviour the focus of any discussion. By doing this, they do not create personal barriers which are sometimes difficult to overcome and which are certainly not conducive to learning.

One of the best ways for a teacher to avoid conflict, maintain authority and obtain the desired behaviours from their pupils is to offer them choices. Let me give you three typical examples. As we all know, mobile phones are commonplace in schools today. Virtually every pupil has one. Although there are obviously many advantages to youngsters having phones, they are the bane of most teachers' lives when they start ringing in class, or when pupils try to make calls or send messages during lessons. Many schools ban them, whilst others simply demand that the pupils do not use these during lesson time.

The sanctions in my particular school are straightforward; if a phone rings or pupils try to make calls, then the phone is to be confiscated. Whilst I agree that persistent offenders should be dealt with firmly and in accordance with the rules, I do feel that there is leeway for alternative action. If this happens in my classroom, I simply say something like 'Lauren, you know what the rules about mobile phones are and you have a choice. You can either switch the phone off, put it in your bag, or you can give it to me and come to collect it at the end of the day'. I have generally found this method to be highly successful. By adopting this approach, I have both maintained my authority, reinforced the school rules and obtained the desired effect of removing the mobile phone from use in the classroom. The important thing to remember is that with this scenario, there has been no stand-off or *impasse* where the pupil has felt pushed into a corner. By giving the pupil a choice, both parties are able to keep their dignity. The same choice-giving method can be applied to pupils listening to personal stereos, wearing trainers and so on.

My other example relates to misbehaviour in lessons. Think about a situation where a pupil has overstepped the mark as far as their behaviour is concerned. You have given them several warnings, but these have remained unheeded. At this point, you need to give them a choice in the actions they take. You could say something to the pupil like this. 'Teresa, you know the rules about distracting others. You are not allowing the people around you to concentrate. I have spoken to you about this before, but as you have ignored my warnings, I am giving you a choice of actions. You can either move to the front of the class, or you can work on your own outside.'

Have you ever been in a situation where a pupil simply will not obey your instructions? I certainly have, and probably will be again at some point before I retire. Perhaps you have asked a pupil to move from one seat to another, or to leave the room, and they have simply refused to budge. It is one of those stand-off situations again where time seems to stand still, where you feel the eyes of every pupil focusing on you, and where you think to yourself: one of us has got to back down here. This situation is all about power! Again, giving choices in situations such as these, can often diffuse potential conflict, get you both off the hook, and maintain your credibility in front of the other pupils. You need to adopt a calm and non-aggressive tone of voice, and say something like: 'Fair enough, Michael, I can't make you move

– in the end that's down to you, but you do have a choice here. Either you move now, or I will have to catch up with you in your free time so that we can discuss it later. What do you think?' I have found that, in most cases, the desired outcome has been achieved. In situations where youngsters have failed to comply with my instructions, I have told them that I will be calling for them when the heat has died down. I have then collected them from their lessons just before the morning or dinner-time break so that I can talk to them in their own time about the issue.

One of the things I focused on in my previous book (2003) is the issue of pupils' secondary behaviour. When a teacher gets seduced away from the initial disciplinary issue and starts to focus on the subsequent inappropriate behaviour of the pupil, then conflict is likely to arise. The best way to explain this is to give you a typical example. A teacher notices Hannah passing a note across the table to Darren when they are supposed to be taking a test under examination conditions. 'Bring the note here please, Darren.' The whole class stops work to look at Darren, who grins, stands up and swaggers over to the front of the class. As he walks past Ashley, he playfully hits him on the back of the head. 'Ouch!' shouts Ashley. The rest of the pupils start laughing. Darren is in his element – a captive audience – great! He then screws the note up and flings it basketball style on to the teacher's desk. There is no doubt that Darren's behaviour, subsequent to the note-passing incident, is unacceptable, but there are two ways the teacher can react here. In this first scenario the teacher focuses on Darren's secondary behaviour and challenges him on three counts, even before he tackles the primary cause of his displeasure, that is, the irregular communication during an examination. The teacher yells at Darren for grinning disrespectfully at him. As a result of this, Darren rolls his eyes and scowls back at him 'God, I was only smiling! There's no law against that is there?' 'Don't be insolent, Darren, or I'll give you a detention.' Then the teacher reacts angrily when he sees Ashley being hit by Darren. 'Leave Ashley alone, Darren, he's done nothing to you.' 'Yes, he has', says Ashley. 'He called me a loser for not being able to do the test.' 'Well, perhaps you are a loser if someone has to pass you a note with the answer on it!' shouts the teacher. 'I'm not the loser! – You're the loser, you're really sad!' shouts Darren. The final straw occurs when Darren really takes the mickey by throwing the paper on to the teacher's desk. 'Right, that's it, Darren! Enough is enough – get out of my room – I will not accept such insolence! Go down to the head of year. He can sort you out!'

Ask yourself – who has really won in a situation such as this? The working week in a school is absolutely littered with incidents such as these, where teachers have become embroiled in the secondary behaviour of pupils. The mistake that this teacher made was to focus entirely on Darren's secondary behaviour and to ignore the primary issue. I am not saying that his inappropriate behaviour should not be challenged. However, this could have been done at a later point and in a less aggressive fashion. By doing this, the issue could also have been discussed without an audience. This teacher needed to focus all his attention on the main issue; that of highlighting the point that pupils have to abide by the regulations set out by examination boards. Earlier on, I advised you not to push pupils into a corner. You should also be very careful not to back *yourself* into one where the only outcome is likely to be conflict. I am sure you will agree that in this particular incident this teacher set himself up for a fall!

Now take time to think about this classroom scenario. Break-time has just finished. The teacher is ready to start the lesson. A young lad with a reputation for being *challenging* brings his football in to the classroom and starts bouncing the ball provocatively on the top of the desk. The teacher walks over to the desk, snatches the ball and takes it to front of the classroom.

Teacher: 'Right, give the ball to me – this isn't the playground.'

Pupil: 'That's not fair! You haven't started the lesson yet!'

Teacher: 'I don't care – you know you shouldn't have brought the ball into the room.'

Pupil: 'You can't do that – it's my ball. You've got no right to take it. It's mine!'

Teacher: 'I can do what I like, I'm the teacher!'

Pupil: 'You're a useless teacher – I hate you!'

Teacher: 'Don't speak to me like that! You need to show some respect!'

Pupil: 'Why should I respect you? Your lessons are … !' (Pupil walks out)

Again, this situation is all about power! Both the teacher and the pupil feel that they want the last word on the issue. However, it is important not to forget who the adult is. It is the teacher's responsebility to recognise what the pupil is trying to do, and to deal with the situation in an authoritative, objective and assertive manner. In this case, however, both parties see the situation as a personal battle and all about *winning* and *losing*. The pupil is deliberately trying to deflect the issue from the original offence, that of bouncing the ball in the classroom. He knows that he was wrong but is upset by the aggressive and autocratic manner in which the teacher has dealt with the issue. He wants to punish the teacher for causing him to lose face in front of his peers. The teacher, on the other hand, has almost forgotten the original issue and is focusing on the rudeness and disrespect of the pupil concerned. He feels that his authority has been threatened in front of the other pupils in the class. Both parties are highly charged emotionally and the situation has reached an *impasse*!

You will remember that earlier in this chapter, we explored ways in which this type of situation can be prevented through the use of an authoritative teaching style. Let us assume that you have done all you can to adopt this approach; you have given this pupil choices; you have spoken in a polite, calm assertive and authoritative manner; you have not pushed him into a corner but have given time to comply with your instructions. Unfortunately, although you are confident that you have done everything by the book on this occasion, this just has not worked. So, again, where do you go from here? There is obviously a need to follow things up with this youngster at some point. My advice would be not to deal with the issue there and then, but to say something like: 'I feel we both need a bit of time away from this. I'll have a chat with you at the end of the lesson.' You may even feel that the youngster needs a longer period of time to calm down. You will have to judge the situation for yourself. However, what is absolutely imperative is that you do come back to the youngster and challenge his or her behaviour.

So far, we have focused on how an authoritative teacher deals with inappropriate pupil behaviour. It is important, though, to bear in mind that there is much more to establishing good working relationships with pupils than just reacting in an appropriate manner to their misbehaviour. A good teacher will scan the classroom, looking for pupils carrying out their assigned tasks, and celebrate pupil success where relevant. An authoritative teacher has enough self-esteem and feels relaxed enough to make good use of humour in the classroom. Most importantly, a good teacher will not be afraid to show his or her human side to pupils. We all get things wrong occasionally and, if you are trying to encourage a high level of reflectivity amongst your pupils, it is important to apologise to them when you get it wrong. When I say 'apologise' I do not mean in a fawning, sycophantic way – that would simply be seen by many pupils to be a sign of weakness. Throughout my career, there have been many occasions where I have overreacted to a pupil's inappropriate behaviour and been too acerbic or robust in my disciplinary responses. In these situations I try very hard to make amends, by asking to see the pupil concerned, and by trying to re-establish good relationships with them. I remember doing this with one particular Year 9 pupil who was really winding me up with some low level, but nevertheless, annoying behaviour. Let us call this pupil John. I remember the lesson well. I was feeling very tired and stressed and things were going quite badly during the lesson. John was not working at his task and laughing at one of his friends. Suddenly I simply snapped. I let John have it! John's misdemeanour was trivial and certainly did not warrant the personal attack I made on him. Since I felt awful about the situation, I knew I had to do something about it. I called John to see me during the afternoon registration session, and apologised for the way that I had spoken to him. I told him that, although his behaviour was unacceptable, I had no right to speak to him like that. John was so taken aback by my apology that I experienced no further problems with him for the rest of that year. In fact, I would go even further than this. This simple apology improved my relationship with this youngster so dramatically that, a year later, he still comes to see me to check if 'I am alright'. You will remember me extolling the virtues of Zimpher and Howey (1987) who described the four domains of teaching and the need for teachers to adopt a balanced approach towards their job. I feel the description of events shown above, together with the summary in Figure 3.3, reflects my effective use of the personal domain. Remember that in this domain,

This teacher focuses on the rights of all pupils to learn.

This teacher uses the strength of their relationships with pupils to gain respect.

This teacher looks for opportunities to praise and to encourage pupils and to celebrate their successes.

This teacher does not verbally attack pupils, but challenges the inappropriateness of their behaviour.

This teacher knows when to ignore tactically inappropriate secondary behaviour.

This teacher uses preventative class management measures to minimise pupil disruption. He or she plans these into their lessons.

This teacher uses respectful lang-uage to the pupils even when angry.

This teacher issues instructions clearly and firmly.

This teacher knows when to apologise.

This teacher does not hold a grudge and tries to re-establish good working relation-ships as soon as possible.

However, it is not as simple as all that!

Do you recognise any of your teaching behaviours here?

Figure 3.3: Characteristics of democratic-authoritative teaching style the conception of teaching is one of a 'self-actualised person' who uses him or herself as an effective and humane instrument of classroom instruction. I feel that I was successful in showing John a number of things – that teachers get things wrong; that it is not a sign of weakness to apologise; that I was right to criticise his behaviour, but wrong to make a personal attack on him; that relationships can be re-built successfully after conflict. Although this was a successful outcome I do not lay claim to getting it right in every situation. But I keep trying!

To sum up

What have we discovered so far in this chapter? We have continued our exploration of the work of Zimpher and Howey (1987), who put forward the idea that a teacher's role should be comprised of four domains: the technical, the clinical, the personal and the critical. I have shown my support for their view that a good teacher should maintain a balance between all four domains and that they should not be over-reliant on any specific one. We have also ascertained that there are teachers with varying degrees of self-esteem and that their level of self-worth can seriously impact on the quality of their teacher/pupil relationships. We have also discussed the classification of three different types of teachers (Lewin *et al.*, 1939) and explored the implications of teaching and management styles on teacher/pupil relationships.

Throughout this chapter, I have asked you, implicitly and, sometimes explicitly, to think about your own sense of *self-worth* and how this may have affected your own teaching style. I have also asked you to consider where you might place yourself along this teaching and management style continuum. However, I am fully aware that, at this point of your career, this may be easier said than done. Adopting this high level of reflectivity is not only intellectually demanding, but is also time-consuming and physically and emotionally exhausting. The process also requires a level of confidence and self-esteem not usually found amongst teachers in their first few years of teaching. Nevertheless, my advice is to start your reflective journey now and simply do what you can under the circumstances. However, do not expect to get it completely right first time! This would be a tall order for even the most experienced and reflective of teachers. Although my confidence levels and my professional sense of worth are pretty high, these do fluctuate quite dramatically at times during the academic year. You may be surprised to know that I am not alone in feeling like this. I gave a lot of attention in my book (Dixie, 2003) to the importance of a teacher's emotional state of mind and confidence levels when starting with their new classes in September. The following quotations from two very experienced teachers show that however long we have been teaching, we all experience peaks and troughs in our emotional state and confidence levels. The first is from a capable and highly respected assistant head of department with twenty-four years experience:

'The night before we return in September I know I am going to sleep badly. I wake up every hour and get up very early even though I know I have got everything ready the night before. I have to force myself to eat and drink as I always feel sick. Once I am at school I feel even sicker. When my classes arrive my mouth goes dry – I never sit down for the first lessons. I suppose I need to look more menacing and, as I am only small, standing when they are sitting seems to make a difference. I go over what they do when arriving to the lesson, what equipment I expect them to have and my expectations of how they should behave etc. I try to get them to give me reasons for rules, and I probably talk for too long! I've had nightmares about arriving a day late for school and about my classes having no teacher for that first day! At the end of the first day I am truly exhausted. I've used up my nervous energy for the next month in one go.' (Dixie, 2003)

This next comes from an extremely efficient and well-respected senior teacher of twenty-five years experience who was, nevertheless, still prepared to expose her vulnerabilities in writing.

'I always feel really nervous before the first day in September. I never sleep well the night before and I don't feel confident when the day arrives (after twenty-five years). I always try to stand in the foyer early in the morning to meet the students as they arrive just to get into the swing of things! When I meet my classes for the first time I feel nervous and unsure of myself. I always go through my routines and what is expected of them but I always try to get a bit of maths in there too so that I get to know their names as soon as possible. Something they can succeed at – nothing too difficult – so that they can go away and look forward to coming back.' (Dixie, 2003)

The reason I have included these two extracts is to show you that the feelings and emotions you may be having now do not go away completely. As you get more experienced, you learn to accept and deal with these and move on. Bearing in mind that you, as beginning teachers, are still learning the trade and do not have the same cushion of experience to fall back on, you are more likely to experience emotional extremes. I have spoken to many beginning teachers who have felt absolute *elation* and *despair* all within the same lesson! There is also no doubt that a teacher's emotional state can have direct consequences on the way he or she relates to their pupils. As we have already discussed, teachers with a lack of confidence tend to be irritable, to snap at youngsters and to overreact to incidents that occur in their classrooms. Whenever this has happened to me, I have apologised to the pupils concerned and explained to them that I am 'having a bad day', asking them to understand my situation. This however only works if you do the same for them, when they too are struggling with their self-esteem and confidence levels.

So how do you become the type of teacher you aspire to be? How do you become more confident? How do you learn to control your emotional state? My response to these questions is quite simple: with an open mind, with a willingness to celebrate your own strengths, with an acceptance of your own shortcomings and with a great deal of effort! I advise beginning teachers to keep a reflective log in which they can record their feelings, emotions, and the events that have occurred within their working week. Keeping a log during the initial

stages of your teaching career can help you to learn from your experiences, and can serve to show you how far you have really come during your time in the school. You are also advised to find a *critical friend* with whom you can be totally honest in sharing your thoughts, feelings and emotions. If you are fortunate enough, this person could turn out to be your mentor, but this does not necessarily have to be the case. The sort of person you need to confide in is someone who is non-judgemental, who has a full grasp of the reflective process and someone who fully understands the link between a teacher's self-esteem and the quality of their relationships with pupils.

Chapter 4

What do They Think of Us?
– a pupil's perspective

It is fair to say that in the distant past the teacher/pupil relationship equation was straightforward. The teacher was there to teach, to pass on knowledge; and the pupil was there to learn, to be the passive recipient of that knowledge. Generally speaking, there was limited interaction between the two parties.

Since the 1980s, however, schools have changed significantly in their attempts to reflect the changing values of society and there is a strong feeling that education has become far more market-orientated, or client-based, in its function. Manifestations of this can be seen in such governmental initiatives as open enrolment, league tables, and OFSTED inspections. The growth of pupil-centred learning in primary and secondary schools means that individual pupil needs have now become a far more important factor in the educational equation. In an attempt to cope with this seed change, many teachers have had to re-appraise their attitudes and roles. The responsibilities of newly qualified teachers today, for example, call for them to display a whole gamut of skills such as co-ordination, monitoring, negotiation, group-structuring, and resource and personnel management. Obviously, in order to meet these requirements, the teacher has to be able to display certain characteristics sympathetic to this method of working and to the increasing amount of pupil/teacher interaction required in the modern day classroom. It is the premise of this chapter, therefore, that knowledge of pupils' perceptions of a good teacher will help teachers in their everyday practice. Such knowledge will give teachers a clearer picture of pupil expectations and guide their teaching behaviours in the classroom.

'Hang on a minute,' I hear you say, 'I am not here to pander to the needs of my pupils. Schools should not be likened to superstores, where people can simply walk in and pick and choose what they want off the shelf. Of course, I will do my best to interest and stimulate the pupils, but I am here to teach and they will simply have to take it or leave it.' I am afraid that my reply to this view is robust. The reality of the situation in most schools today is that, unless you do take the needs and wants of pupils fully into consideration, instead of *taking it*, your pupils *will* simply *leave it*.

As we have mentioned on numerous occasions, good teacher/ pupil relationships lie at the very heart of successful teaching. Good teachers show awareness and an understanding of the interactions that take place between them and their pupils. Good teachers listen to what their pupils have to say and to what they want. This does not mean that they are constantly acquiescing to the whims or demands of these youngsters, but they do listen and, where possible, they do modify their teaching behaviours accordingly. Understanding the 'how', 'what' and 'why' of the way pupils think, helps us to interact positively with them in the classroom. Kutnik and Jules (1988) put this notion extremely succinctly:

Knowledge of pupils' perceptions therefore, allows others into the world of pupils' realities – realities which are frequently the source of their beliefs and in turn their behaviours.

It is interesting to note that even in the early twentieth century there were some enlightened educational pioneers who explored the importance of understanding the interactive nature of the classroom. These words offered by James Ward (1926), cited in Taylor (1962), provide the core tenet of this chapter.

Surely one of the first steps towards the understanding of the young is to know how they regard us.

So where does this leave you as beginning teachers? What must you do to find out about the perceptions of the pupils in your classes? To help you do this, allow me to describe a piece of low-level research I carried out for my first degree.

My preliminary research provided plenty of evidence to suggest strongly that the personal characteristics of the teacher make a considerable difference to pupil behaviour, motivation and achievement. I wanted to look at the characteristics of the teacher from the perspective of their pupils, and to find out exactly how these affected pupil behaviour and educational output. To explore this topic I decided to use two main research methods. The first involved a free-response essay-type exercise where Year 8 pupils were simply asked to describe the characteristics of their favourite teachers. Their responses were analysed using content analysis. The second method took on a more quantitative stance, and involved using a 'Likert' style questionnaire designed to find a correlation between the perceptions of pupils of their teachers, and the amount of effort they made in lessons. For the purposes of this chapter, however, I am going to focus on the pupils' essay responses, because it is predominantly these findings that have subsequently had such a great influence on my teaching behaviour.

Although I feel it is unnecessary to explore further the rationale or methodology of this research in any great detail, I do need to include just one piece of additional information, that in the initial stages the pupils from this specific subject group and I spent some time negotiating a common view of the following teacher characteristics:

- Conscientiousness
- Enthusiasm
- Friendliness
- Confidence
- Humour
- Sensitivity

It was important for us to do this in order to ensure that every pupil had a similar understanding of what was meant by the various teacher characteristics listed above. I chose these specific qualities as a focus for exploration since they represented the main teacher characteristics, described in my background reading. Allow me to share the views of a few of these pupils concerning their teachers.

'Conscientiousness' came highest on the list of preferred teacher qualities. Comments relating to a teacher's conscientiousness included references to the teacher being prepared to explain tasks in detail and using strategies tapered to meet all pupils' needs. A number of pupils felt it was important that the teacher stayed in the classroom and did not disappear for any length of time, feeling that continued teacher absence from the classroom was extremely de-motivating. A number felt that teachers should make strenuous efforts to ensure that their pupils recorded their homework tasks, which should be marked regularly. Failure to do so, they said, would result in poor pupil effort in subsequent assignments. One pupil put his case quite vehemently:

> 'When you've got homework and you've tried your best, you want to get it marked, don't you? This is an important thing you must do.'

Another pupil actually quantified the exact amount of homework a pupil of their age should do, quoting extracts from the school's homework policy. This was supported by another pupil who stated that:

> 'The teacher should take the books in on a regular basis so that all marking is kept up to date. For example, teacher X may take pupils' books in and keep marking up to date, so if there are pupils who are having difficulties, these problems can be sorted out. Teacher Y may hardly ever take books in to mark so some pupils who are struggling may never be helped unless they have the courage to ask.'

A substantial number of pupils mentioned that a good teacher is thoroughly prepared for lessons with as many external stimuli as possible, (videos, audio tapes, slides, etc.), one saying about this:

'I think a teacher who has given a lot of thought to the lesson and knows what he or she is going to say or do makes a lesson go more smoothly.'

Some of the pupils wrote about the importance of the teacher insisting upon a good standard of work. One pupil in particular said:

'If a pupil's work is messy then I think that the teacher who is teaching should make them do it again. If the pupil hasn't done their work then I think the teacher should give them a detention.'

It would seem that from the number of times pupils mentioned some aspect of conscientiousness it features very highly in a pupil's expectations of a good teacher. My secondary research confirmed a direct link between the conscientiousness of teachers and the work-rate, performance and behaviour of their pupils.

Many pupils referred, as those teachers did in Chapter 2, to the importance of teacher enthusiasm in the learning equation.

'If a teacher is enthusiastic about their subject, this enthusiasm will often rub off on their pupils.'

'He or she will encourage me to work hard and be enthusiastic about ideas that I discuss with them.'

One specific pupil took this idea further by explaining what they actually meant by the term 'enthusiasm':

'A teacher should have different tones of voice to make things exciting and also interesting, so you don't fall asleep with boredom in the class. My English teacher from Year 7 sounded exciting when explaining a piece of work and also when reading to the class.'

Another pupil, when talking about the importance of making eye contact as being part of the repertoire of an enthusiastic teacher, carried on to describe the teaching behaviour of a particular teacher:

'The way she conducted the lesson with such ease but so much enthusiasm and she looked her eyes with everyone's and walked in between our
desks involving all pupils.'

Although many of the comments about teacher enthusiasm were not
as well developed as that of teacher conscientiousness, its importance
could be implied from the very context of these comments. Throwa-
way lines such as 'a teacher should be enthusiastic and make the work
sound good and not boring' were common when I was analysing the
results of the research.

What certainly emerged from this exercise was the importance of
teacher warmth and friendliness. One pupil expanded upon this in
some detail by saying:

'Another important quality in a teacher is friendliness. If a teacher is
friendly towards their pupils, the pupils will feel more inclined to talk to
the teacher if they have a personal problem or if they do not understand
the work they have been set.'

Often associated with their description of a *friendly* teacher was that of
cheerfulness, and the two were often taken as synonymous. One pupil
wrote about the importance of friendliness but went on to say that
this, in itself, was not enough. They expected the teacher to be friendly
but firm, so that real learning could take place in a relaxed atmosphere. It also seemed to be extremely important to the pupils that
teachers made them feel welcome when they entered the classroom.
One pupil took this a stage further by describing the type of teacher
behaviour that made him or her feel welcome:

'Another thing I find welcoming in the lesson is when your teacher
speaks your language like "Hi! – you all right?" and things like that. That
makes the lesson feel more comfortable because you know that he or she
is stooping down to your level just to make you feel welcome.'

The secondary data used in this study went a long way to supporting
the essence of this primary research.

Classifying teacher confidence was quite difficult. Where pupils
had not overtly mentioned this term, I had to infer the importance of
this from their descriptions of what I saw to be the behaviour of a

confident teacher in terms of class control and in dealing firmly but fairly with pupils. Comments such as the one shown below help to exemplify my point:

'Teachers should always maintain a good level of discipline with pupils in the class. This is important because you know the teacher is in charge but you can still have a laugh and it does not get out of hand.'

A number of pupils take this line; some go on to mention that unless this firmness is achieved in the classroom, then little or no work will be carried out. Some pupils went on to mention overtly the import-ance of confidence and how a lack of confidence, often displayed by inexperienced teachers, can lead to a breakdown in discipline and disrupt learning.

As expected, a sense of humour was extremely important to pupils. They felt that a teacher's ability to display a good sense of humour made the atmosphere in the class a happy one. One pupil referred to the importance of the teacher being able to take a joke, and stressed the importance of the teacher being funny. He went on to say:

'I do not mean joke telling. I mean saying something funny on the spur of the moment or taking the micky out of someone; e.g. a slide of an old car and saying it is a particular teacher's car.'

One pupil, when talking about humour and teachers who motivated him, said:

'I hate boring teachers – that just makes me bored and so I don't listen and so I don't do any work.'

Teacher sensitivity could cover a multitude of behaviour. For the purpose of this exercise it was taken to mean an obvious sympathy for the individual's physical, emotional, social and mental well-being. An element of *caring* was, therefore, involved here. One pupil, writing about the importance of a teacher caring, stated:

'I feel this is important because each pupil needs to feel they are im-portant. Each pupil has different abilities, and a caring teacher will always consider this and give positive criticisms to these pupils.'

Many pupils wrote about how important it was for the teacher to be sympathetic towards those in difficulty, as well as the necessity for teachers to listen to pupils' problems. Real learning, they said, cannot take place if pupils are unhappy. What immediately became obvious when analysing the findings of the pupil questionnaires, was how sophisticated many of the responses were from these young people, and how astute their observations were of our performances in the classroom. The question that needed asking, however, was whether older children view their teachers in a similar fashion. It was with precisely this question in mind that I carried out a survey of pupil perceptions of good teachers with a hundred Year 10 and 11 pupils. The rationale behind this was to ascertain whether those extra couple of years made any difference in terms of their views on teaching behaviours. What immediately became glaringly evident was that the majority of these older pupils recognised the fine balance that teachers need to strike between showing humour, warmth, care and concern, and maintaining good order in their classrooms.

The findings of this research showed me that a teacher's ability to control classes proved to be an increasingly dominant pre-requisite as these youngsters moved into adolescence. Some of the views of the pupils have been offered below:

'Teacher X is a strict teacher but is very good as he makes us learn. They have a good personality and you can get along with them.'

'Teacher X keeps the class under control and makes the lesson interesting and doesn't make the class bored.'

'This teacher is strict and keeps his pupils under control without fail. If he is in a good mood, you will have a fun lesson and enjoy it. This teacher is respected by all, not because he is strict, but because he has earned it.'

'A good teacher is someone who can keep a class under control and makes the work interesting. I think that they have a sense of humour, is someone who listens, who helps you to understand things better. Every teacher must have rules but not be too strict.'

'Teacher X has a good personality who has his own rules. These rules are not too harsh. They are not strict but can keep the class under control.

Their lesson is ready and well prepared for when you basically walk into the classroom.'

'I think a good teacher is someone who is strict but also has a laugh with you every now and again. You know they actually want to teach you and that they are always positive and help you when you are stuck.'

'Teacher X is good teacher because they are not afraid to send out any trouble-makers so that the rest of the class can work. They also joke about with the class so that the pupils can have a nice working environment. Teacher X can get serious with the class and make them work in silence but normally they will let us talk during the lesson. Overall, teacher X is humorous and is a good laugh.'

A sense of humour and teacher warmth continued to be important pre-requisites of a good teacher, but *only* when combined with their ability to control the class. About 95 per cent of the respondents in the survey mentioned the teacher's need to have a sense of humour and to be able to laugh with their pupils. The comments below provide a flavour of the research findings.

'Teacher X is a very good teacher for two reasons. They manage to keep control of their classes but still maintain a good sense of humour. They like to have a good laugh and joke.'

'A good teacher has a laugh with the class but we still learn things.'

'A good teacher has a lot of charisma and a good sense of humour.'

However, it is not as straightforward as this. I mentioned above that older pupils can recognise the need for a *balanced* approach by teachers. The following comments by Year 11 pupils exemplify this.

'A bad teacher tries to be funny but simply isn't.'

'A good teacher doesn't always have to be the centre of attention.'

Also particularly interesting about these findings was that as the pupils moved into adolescence they identified good teachers as being good listeners and being there for them to talk to. We need to re-member that this is a particularly traumatic time for many young people and we should never underestimate the need for many of them to talk to adults other than their parents.

'Teacher X is an excellent teacher because he is a very reliable, kind and valuable teacher to have around. The respect I have for him is like no other teacher I have had. I have learned so much from him and he is always around for me to talk to and I know he will help me with any problem.'

'Teacher X is an excellent teacher. She is well-respected and kind and helps a lot. She is always there for helpful advice. She is more like a friend than a teacher. She is one of us!'

However, kindness and consideration do not seem to be enough for many pupils as they move up into their examination years. For example, many pupils described some of their teachers as being kind but went on to mention how ineffective they were in the classroom. The following comments from two Year 11 pupils get the point across.

'Teacher X is a kind teacher but goes through things too fast for me to understand the information properly.'

'Teacher X is okay but needs to control the class more. She waits too long and pupils get bored and mess about … Teacher X is a nice teacher but needs to be in control of what the class are doing and to set work to do so that they get stuck into it. Teacher X needs to set something interesting so that the class don't become a nuisance.'

When you come to read Chapter 6, you will understand that as many children move into adolescence their boredom threshold is likely to become significantly lower. Whilst these pupils wanted their teachers to be firm, fair and fun, they were also a lot more demanding about teaching styles employed. Besides the traits described above, many older pupils made comments related to teaching and learning issues, for example, about the ability and willingness of teachers to explain things clearly; to make themselves accessible when youngsters were experiencing difficulties; to introduce a variety of teaching and learning styles into lessons; to have a good fund of subject knowledge. The following pupil comments provide a flavour of these views.

'Teacher W is a good teacher because in class you are able to do presentations, that is, radio, video and PowerPoint presentations. You can also do posters and leaflets and this helps us learn because it is more interesting and is easier to learn and to remember things.'

'Teacher W is also a good teacher because at the beginning of each lesson we do a starter activity and so we are prepared for the lesson ahead. Teacher W also has a scheme to motivate pupils. This scheme is the 'student of the month' where a certificate and a postcard are awarded and sent home. This helps to motivate me and everybody else because they want to win the award.'

'Teacher W is also a good teacher because they are not only a good speaker and teacher, but a good listener, friend. Teacher W is a good teacher because you can have a laugh and talk but also have to work.'

'Teacher X motivates his pupils by spending his own money on prizes for project winners.'

'To help pupils he lets them have his own personal details so that they can contact him to receive help whenever they need it. By doing this, they have no excuse for late homework. He gives up his own time if pupils miss lessons.'

'When he teaches he tries different methods, like book methods, group learning and individual projects. He goes over the work again and again until people understand it.'

'A good teacher has a wide subject knowledge and knows how to present it and to keep pupils interested and not to lose their concentration.'

'A good teacher knows what they are talking about.'

'If you are ever stuck he will go over and over it again until you understand. He will listen and explain if you need it. I have never understood this subject so much!'

'A good teacher is someone who doesn't make us bored but who can make the work enjoyable.'

'A good teacher has a *fun* teaching technique.'

'A good teacher helps us to learn in *fun* ways.'

Where have you heard all this before? Yes, you are absolutely right, the descriptions of the characteristics of good teachers offered by these youngsters match up perfectly with the description of the *authoritative* teacher in the previous chapter. So much for the view that teachers should not pander to the whims of their pupils! These pupils are not asking for anything that is going to threaten radically the British educational system. They have been honest enough to recognise that their behaviour needs to be controlled, that most of them need and want to learn, and that there should be mutual respect in the classroom. My message to you as beginning teachers is simple: when you feel secure enough and providing you take care in setting up the context and rules for your research, you must spend time canvassing the opinions of your pupils about what goes on in your classroom. I should warn you, however, that you need to be very clear about what exactly you are trying to find out. You should not use your findings primarily to act as a measure of your popularity, but you should take an opportunity to discover the quality of your teaching and your professional relationships with your pupils. Whilst lesson observation feedback from your colleagues can prove useful in giving you a snapshot of your teaching, the pupils see you teach when you are off your guard, and far more regularly. They will be able to give a broader and more honest perspective of your strengths and weaknesses.

So, how do you find out about your pupils' perceptions of the quality of your teaching? At this point it would be easy for me to walk into my office, take one of my pupil perception questionnaires off the shelf, and simply replicate it below. However, this would be neither fair nor helpful to you. I feel secure enough with my classes to be able to take risks and to ask some quite searching questions of my pupils. I know instinctively when things have been going badly and when they have been going reasonably well. However, I find the use of pupil questionnaires invaluable in providing information that will help me to fine tune and hone my teaching.

Unless you want to open a few wounds you as beginning teachers are going to have to be quite cautious and circumspect in your enquiries. With this advice in mind, I have provided an example of some questionnaire research carried out by a graduate teacher trainee in the second term of his placement at my secondary school (see Figure 4.1). When reading through his questionnaire, you will see how careful he was in his use of language. He encouraged his pupils to be constructive and objective in their comments and so reduced the likelihood of them making insulting and negative personal remarks. You will also notice how he 'de-personalised' the process, by focusing the attention of the pupils on a number of issues relating to a specific unit of work, rather than solely on him as their teacher. True, in a subtle and round about way, he canvassed the opinions of his pupils on his teaching, but this was done in a wider context of learning and teaching issues associated with this unit of work. It is also pleasing to see that the questionnaire was by no means a one-way process. There were ample opportunities for the pupils themselves to be reflective about their own performances and contributions.

Using surveys such as this is important for two reasons. First, they can furnish us with information about our teaching behaviours, and about the quality of our lessons. In doing so, they can help us to make informed decisions about our practice. The second but nevertheless equally important reason is that this process can really help to increase pupil ownership of their learning. They really appreciate being listened to. The young graduate teacher described the way both the standard of his teaching and the quality of his relationships with his pupils, in this potentially challenging class, improved dramatically in the period after he had carried out this exercise. You do need to be aware, however, that there is a big risk involved in carrying out an activity such as this. No matter how hard you try to get the pupils to be constructive in their comments, you must always be prepared to hear things you do not particularly want to hear. I felt this young man to be extremely brave in carrying out this survey at such an early stage in his teaching career. Many beginning teachers would, understandably, be a little more reluctant to ask such searching questions.

Difficult as it is, it is imperative that we do ask questions like these if we want to improve the learning scenarios for our pupils. The accepted view of teaching is that success in the classroom depends very much on the quality of the teacher/pupil interaction. Sometimes harmonious interaction occurs naturally when our characteristics or personality traits coincide with the specific requirements of the pupils. At other times, modification of styles, behaviour and characteristics needs to occur. Pupils are less likely to modify their behaviour than teachers because (a) they are usually less capable of doing so and (b) because they see it as the teacher's task to motivate them. The crucial questions are, therefore, how far can teachers be trained in effective interaction and how far is it a function of their temperament?

It is fair to say that teachers with certain personality traits will find it easier to adopt a variety of interactional techniques and identify the cues that make certain styles and characteristics desirable. Other teachers will find this more difficult. This chapter has looked specifically at certain teacher characteristics and their effect on the learning process. It is important to say that a good teacher is not a good teacher simply because he or she has certain characteristics, but because of that indefinable *something* that comes into play when the characteristics of that teacher coincide with what is wanted by a particular pupil at that particular time.

What then are the implications of this chapter for those of you who are at the beginning of your careers? If one accepts the premise that the characteristics of a teacher can affect pupil motivation, then there is obviously a need for action. The importance of inter-relational skills should be stressed in all initial teacher training induction programmes and greater emphasis should be placed on the role of pupils as a resource for research into classroom practice. Those of you who are still in your newly qualified teacher induction, or training years, need to be proactive in seeking opportunities to involve your pupils in action-research projects, such as the one described in this chapter. If it is not possible to get involved in grand schemes such as this, simply take opportunities every day to talk to your pupils, and to discover their perceptions of the way things are going in your lessons. Having reflected on those perceptions, you then need to decide whether you need to modify your teaching behaviours in any way.

Read the statements and tick the relevant box.

	Strongly agree	Agree	Undecided	Disagree	Strongly disagree
I always work to the best of my ability in class	☐	☐	☐	☐	☐
I can be distracted in class	☐	☐	☐	☐	☐
I sometimes distract other people in class	☐	☐	☐	☐	☐
I listen to instructions carefully	☐	☐	☐	☐	☐
I always finish tasks set in class in the lesson	☐	☐	☐	☐	☐
My work is always presented to the best of my ability	☐	☐	☐	☐	☐
I always title and date my work	☐	☐	☐	☐	☐
Worksheets are always stuck into my book and labelled	☐	☐	☐	☐	☐
I always contribute to class discussions and attempt to answer questions	☐	☐	☐	☐	☐
If I am unclear I always ask for help	☐	☐	☐	☐	☐

Figure 4.1: WW1 Evaluation Sheet (continued)

Set yourself two targets to improve your work/effort next term:

1.

2.

What elements of the course have you enjoyed? Why?

What part of the course have you not enjoyed? Why?

Are there any topics that you would have liked o have studied which we did not or did not study in depth? (E.g. Battles, Technology, Shell Shock, Women at War, Eastern Front, Poetry, Aircraft etc. ...)

Read the statements and tick the relevant box.

	Strongly agree	Agree	Undecided	Disagree	Strongly disagree
The teacher explained tasks clearly	☐	☐	☐	☐	☐
The teacher explained key terms and incidents clearly and in a way that was easy to understand	☐	☐	☐	☐	☐
The teacher always gave guidance when it was required	☐	☐	☐	☐	☐
When marking books the teacher's feedback was helpful	☐	☐	☐	☐	☐
Tasks set were interesting and improved your understanding of the Great War	☐	☐	☐	☐	☐

Figure 4.1: WW1 Evaluation Sheet (continued)

What activities would you like to see in lessons that would improve your enjoyment and motivation in Humanities? Please tick: -

More debates:

More role play:

More stimulating activities such as video's, games, quizzes:

More individual research:

More group work:

Other:

Figure 4.1: WW1 Evaluation Sheet

Chapter 5

Creating a Positive Classroom Ethos

Since the late 1990s a great deal of attention has been given to brain-based learning, and quite rightly so. Anything that helps teachers to understand how pupils learn should be given credence. Not so much attention, however, has been paid to how our knowledge of the

brain can help us to establish, maintain and develop good relationships with pupils. This chapter briefly explores the various functions of the brain and goes on to outline how we can use this knowledge to create a positive classroom ethos to manage our classes and improve our relationships with pupils.

Dr Paul MacLean of the National Institute of Mental Health in Washington DC developed a theory which suggested that the human brain can be divided into three distinct areas which he named as:

- the neo-cortex
- the limbic system
- the reptilian brain

See Figure 5.1 for more detailed information.

The neo-cortex can be found at the top of the brain and functions as the cognitive or thinking area. It is divided into two hemispheres and joined by the corpus callosum. This part of the brain is used to solve problems and to identify patterns. The limbic system deals with the emotions, beliefs and value systems and concerns itself with the long-term memory of the person. However, it is the oldest evolutionary part of the brain that provides the main focus for this chapter. I

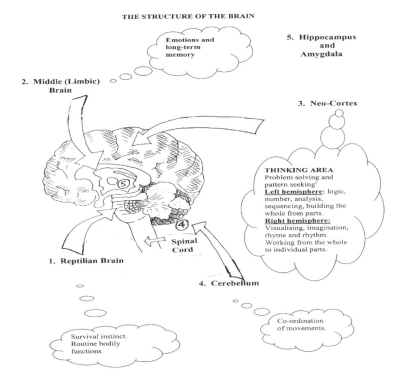

Figure 5.1: The structure of the brain

believe knowledge of the reptilian brain to be of real relevance to the purpose of this book – that of offering advice and guidance on how to establish, maintain and develop good working relations with pupils.

So what do we know about the function of the reptilian brain? It is responsible for routine bodily functions such as breathing, heart-beat, blood pressure and balance. It is the primeval part of the brain that takes charge of our survival responses. The reptilian brain helps us to judge whether to stay and fight in times of danger, or cut our losses and run. Just as in the animal world the reptilian brain predisposes us to a system of social conformity, of being able to know one's place in the pecking order of things and possessing the need to respond to ritualistic rules. In situations where the individual feels threatened, the reptilian brain takes over from the other two areas, and the higher order functions of the brain lose their significance. It is vital too for us to have a full understanding of the role of the reptilian brain if we want the youngsters in our classes to learn.

Creating a physical environment that provides pupils with adequate light, heat, seating space and the opportunity to drink fluids, will go a long way to making your pupils feel safe, secure, happy and ready to learn. If this is done as a matter of course, the pupils will be totally unaware of why they feel more comfortable in your classes. Take these conditions away, however, and you will soon notice a difference in their attitudes and behaviour. More and more schools are allowing their pupils to drink in class so you need to find out what the

policy is in your school. I am lucky enough to have a sink in my classroom, so as long as they ask my permission, pupils are allowed to get themselves a drink. Juice and water are allowed, but cola is banned!

Important though these physical prerequisites of learning are, it is mainly on the emotional conditions of the classroom that I want to focus in this chapter. In order to produce a class of pupils who are happy and in a frame of mind to learn, teachers have to plan for the emotional needs of their charges. They must therefore reduce scenarios that create anxiety, fear, lack of self-esteem, a feeling of isolation, insecurity and a sense of injustice. In short, teachers need to reduce pupil stress. You can do this through an understanding of the role of the hidden curriculum in your classroom. So what exactly is meant by this term 'hidden curriculum'?

The hidden curriculum is a set of values, attitudes and knowledge frames embodied in the organisation and processes of schooling and which are implicitly conveyed to pupils. Two such elements of the hidden curriculum that are relevant to this chapter are that of classroom displays and teacher/pupil interactions.

My advice to you, as beginning teachers, is to take this information on board when you are planning the physical layout of your classroom. I suspect that even the most motivated and positive of teachers do not plan their classroom displays with the reptilian brain in mind. The point I want to make strongly here is that you can do a great deal to cater for the needs of your pupils, even before you start formally teaching them. I have provided you with a few examples from my own classroom.

One of the most important messages I want to get across to my pupils is that it is perfectly alright to get things wrong. I believe that taking risks is an integral part of the learning process, but that this will not happen in a competitive learning environment. To establish a collaborative ethos in the classroom, I have displayed a number of posters with important messages. The first of these messages is that it is 'OK to be wrong!' (Dixie, 1998; 2003). Displayed immediately below this poster, is a building block model which visually demonstrates the need for my pupils to work together to solve problems (Figure 5.2).

At the beginning of the year, I explain to my pupils that each wrong answer given in lessons should be seen as a stimulus (or building block) for other pupils to take on the thought process that bit further. By doing this, an incorrect response is still given a degree of

Figure 5.2:   It's OK to be wrong

status! Each partially correct response acts as a building block for pupils to develop their thought patterns further, and brings the class that bit closer to the desired outcome. I emphasise that the process is to be seen as *collaborative* and not individualistic. Using this approach has had a dramatic effect on my relationships with pupils. They are more willing to get involved, to talk to me, to ask me questions and, most importantly, much more prepared *to take risks* in lessons. So, why exactly does this happen? It is simply because they do not feel threatened! Using this particular model can also help to reduce dramatically discipline problems during lessons (Dixie, 2003).

Simply by putting up posters in the classroom encouraging pupils to take risks, provides them with a sense of security. Explaining to the pupils that you will always be there to catch them if they fall, helps to provide them with the security they need to take those risks so vital to their academic and social development. I feel that the following quotation from a Year 10 pupil really captures the flavour of what I am trying to say.

'When I arrived in the classroom, I felt insecure, but as I settled and looked around, I saw many pictures, posters and signs which help me to understand what is involved by being in the class. Pupils feel shy when they put their hands up, just in case they get it wrong. But in this class there are signs that say "Take a risk" so it is much easier and less threatening when there is something telling you to take a risk and put your hand up.'

It is also important for youngsters to realise that making mistakes is all part of the learning process. You need to inform them that you are doing your best to provide an environment where they feel comfortable in showing their vulnerabilities. I use a couple of traditional Chinese proverbs displayed in my classroom to get over the notion of using failure as a means to success.

Failure lies not in falling down but in not getting up. (Traditional)

He who asks a question is a fool for five minutes. But he who does not ask remains a fool forever. (Traditional)

At the start of the academic year, I show my pupils a draft copy of one of my early MA assignments. The paper is literally covered with the red biro scrawls made by my tutor. The idea behind this is to show the class that even adults have to go through this critical process during their lives. I then go on to say that, providing this critical process takes place in a secure environment, they are likely to come out all the stronger for it. Hopefully, knowing this gives the youngsters in my classes some added security.

I am sure you will agree that raising the self-esteem of pupils has got to be a major aim of any committed teacher. However, how many of you have actually thought of making this message overt? When pupils enter my classroom, they are met with the following message pegged up on a washing line in front of them.

☞ **This is a 'can do' classroom** ☜

This seems pretty basic, doesn't it? However, I assure you that it works! Have a look at this observation made by another Year 10 pupil about the culture of this classroom.

'When you walk into the room all the work on the walls shows that it is a hardworking room. The first banner on the wall – "This is a 'can do' classroom" – shows that the teacher is enthusiastic and wants us to do well. All the displays have obviously had a lot of work put into them and this tells us the teacher works hard to create a good working atmosphere. In Mr Dixie's room I want to work hard because we can tell that he works hard for us and it is only right that we do the same! The room makes me enthusiastic and gives me a positive attitude towards work.'

As a committed teacher, I feel it is important that pupils do their best in my lessons. You must feel the same about your classes. Again, had you thought about making your message more obvious? Setting the scene by displaying motivational posters, such as the one shown below, goes a long way to getting across to your pupils exactly what you expect of them. Providing pupils with firm expectations and clear parameters can help to cater for the reptilian brain.

☞ **Work with pride!** ☜

Never underestimate the use of primary colours and creative displays in promoting warmth and purpose in your classroom! Bright reds, complimented by an array of green plants for example, can go a long way to create a purposeful and stimulating atmosphere, and can convey to the pupils that they are here to work. Perhaps my most successful classroom display has been on the Great War. This particular display consists of numerous photographs, artefacts and pupils' poetry displayed on a background of poppy-red and white paper.

Because of the time allocated to my role as professional development tutor, I do not now get the chance to teach many lower school pupils. However, I enjoy inviting Year 7 and 8 pupils into my room when I am covering for colleagues. I like to watch the expressions on their faces as they enter the classroom. When I hear comments such as 'This is a brilliant classroom, sir!' or '*Cor*, look at those photographs and that war helmet', I know that I have already got these pupils on my side. It is a brilliant feeling and one that I can recommend. In order to provide a pupil perspective on this issue, I have furnished you with a number of pupil quotations below. I feel these say it all.

'When I enter the classroom first thing in the morning, I feel a sudden sense of security. Everywhere I look there is advice and information to help me through my work. The room also has a natural side to it with the plants in the corner and I like that feeling in a classroom. I prefer a classroom which makes a person feel good.'

'When I enter this room, I feel very welcome. There are many colourful posters and motivational quotes. It makes me feel comfortable and willing to work. If the teacher has put in a great deal of effort making this room welcoming, I feel I must put in a great deal of effort into the work he sets me.'

'This classroom makes me feel welcome and because a lot of effort and time have been put into it I will put effort and time into my work. It makes me motivated and gives the teacher respect as well as gives the room respect.'

Youngsters love teachers with a sense of humour, liking jokes no matter how bad they are. They particularly like those made at the expense of other members of staff. Luckily I teach in a school where the camaraderie amongst the teaching staff is absolutely superb and the majority of teachers are well able to enjoy a joke at their own expense. As a result of this, pupil/teacher relationships are some of the best I have experienced in my career. I have scattered my classroom with pages of jokes adapted to suit the characteristics of some of my friends and colleagues. Obviously, it is advisable to request their permission before you do this.

I accept that in the current climate of political correctness, I could be subject to some criticism here. I also accept that in the wrong context, using humour in such a personal way could promote a climate of vindictiveness and bullying amongst the pupils. However, you need to know that I have also displayed a number of visual jokes around the classroom that are very much at *my* expense. I have been successful in using these to help the pupils to take themselves less seriously and to be able to laugh at themselves. I have, therefore, found that far from causing inflammatory situations, using self-deprecatory humour in this mild fashion has often helped to defuse some potentially difficult situations.

When I was studying for my Masters degree, I was extremely impressed by the approach taken by my university tutors towards my learning. The tutors placed a great deal of emphasis on the holistic synthesis of mind, body and emotions; we spent a great deal of time exploring the feelings associated with learning, as well as the subject content of the course. These feelings and emotions were recorded formally in my learning journal. This humanist approach, inspired by the work of Carl Rogers, was obviously an integral part of the learning programme. I like to think I have adopted this approach wherever possible in my teaching. In my opinion, the most successful teachers do not teach subjects – they teach children. By that I mean that they are mainly concerned with the all-round development of youngsters as human beings, and not just as empty receptacles into which knowledge has to be poured. Humanist teachers place an emphasis on the personal growth of their pupils and on their awareness of their place in the world. The purpose of a humanist teacher is to develop a moral and social conscience in young people within their charge. To achieve this, pupils need to be able to make choices and to take responsibility for their decisions. They can do this by being given opportunities to evaluate their thoughts, words and actions, and by being provided with active learning scenarios which can be offered, at a conscious level, through formal curriculum assignments or, at an unconscious level, through the process of pupil/teacher interaction and classroom display material.

With this in mind, I have littered my classroom with opportunities for incidental and unconscious moral and social learning. I have displayed quotations and messages on the backs of all the chairs as well as on the walls, in the firm belief that the pupils will gradually subsume the meaning of these messages whilst they are in my room. I have come into the classroom on many occasions to find youngsters discussing these, some of which I have included below.

Seek friends who are better than you, not your own kind. (Traditional)

Failure is the mother of success. (Traditional)

Once a word is spoken, four horses cannot drag it back. (Traditional)

Only when you know why you have hit the target, can you say you have truly learned archery. (Guan Yinzi)

Any doubts I may have felt about the value of doing this were soon dispelled when I read through the following joint comments made about my classroom by two Year 10 boys.

'This classroom makes us feel welcome and secure. There are many different displays and little speeches. You are bound to learn something even if it is not to do with the lesson. There are laminated quotes which don't make sense at first but, once you think about it they do make sense. They all help people in the world.'

One thing I advise my beginning teachers to do is to spend five minutes or so in their classroom sitting at a desk, and looking at the room from a pupil's perspective. Only by doing this will you be able to understand fully the potential of the classroom for unconscious and incidental learning. To exemplify this further, I asked three beginning teachers to come into my classroom, to imagine that they were pupils and to describe the room from a pupil's perspective. The results have been recorded below:

'When you enter Gererd's room, there is an immediate sense of someone who cares about the students who go in there. The room is brightly coloured and airy. There are plenty of quirky objects to look at and no end of thought-provoking mantras dotted here, there and everywhere. These really help you to believe in yourself and also provide a welcome but harmless visual distraction for those who cannot concentrate for long periods of time.

My favourite part of Gererd's room is his wall display on World War One. Every time I go in, I cannot stop looking at all the textures, photos and snippets of information that it offers. There is even a real rusty old helmet hanging from an amazing display.

This is a room where positive things are expected to happen and where pupils are clearly encouraged to enjoy the whole process of learning.' (Trainee teacher – English)

'When I walk into Mr Dixie's classroom, I am faced with – this is a can do classroom. I remember that it is OK to be wrong here and that if I make a mistake it doesn't matter. We are here to learn and even though it's last thing on a Friday afternoon I still sit and think about what it must have been like to have been in the trenches during the war. I wonder how Mr

Dixie got all that barbed wire on to the wall without hurting himself. Did they really wear those old tin hats?' (Newly qualified teacher – English)

'Walking into a classroom for the first time can be a daunting experience; after all you are entering new territory where you are yet to find your own space. Mr Dixie's class, in this sense, is no different. However, once you have entered the classroom you notice there is almost information overload! At first your eyes are drawn to the various posters depicting everything from pictures of the First World War trenches to posters of Ipswich Town football club, then you realise that some of the pictures are of Mr Dixie and the pupils from the school. This makes you feel more at ease and relaxed. The backs of the chairs are covered with quotes and anecdotes and even jokes. All of a sudden the classroom doesn't seem as daunting as it did a few minutes ago.

The layout of the desks makes it easy to move around the room, all the resources that you need are clearly labelled and easy to find making the room "user" friendly. The overall feel of the classroom is warm and friendly – if your mind starts to wander you find yourself reading one of the quotes or examining a picture which makes it easier to refocus your mind. A "washing line" with posters and pictures hangs from one side of the room. It seems that wherever you look you will be drawn to bite-size chunks of information and you can't help but learn something whenever you are in the room.' (Graduate teacher – History)

A study by Kyriacou and Cheng (1993) explored views of over a hundred PGCE students on their attitude towards humanistic teaching in schools. A sample of these students was interviewed later in the year, once they had completed their first teaching practice in schools. Whereas the vast majority of the original students in the study had agreed with the humanist approach, most of those interviewed after their initial teaching practice had finished said that they found it diffi- cult to put these qualities into practice and to maintain a positive regard for all the pupils in their classes. In other words, they found that the realities of classroom life and the behaviour of the pupils in lessons led them to temper their humanistic approach towards their teaching and to take on a more autocratic role. My role, as profession- al development tutor in a large secondary school, substantiates these findings. In some initial weekly seminars with my beginning teachers, many often express frustration and disappointment with the fact that their pupils do not seem to be responding to their humanist teaching approach. 'The kids are simply not being reasonable!' It is beginning to dawn on them that children are not always reasonable and rational beings; they do not always respond positively to this rather idealistic teaching method. These teachers want me to tell them exactly what is missing from their lessons, and what they need to do to get more disciplined and orderly behaviour from their pupils. I do my best to allay their concerns by telling them that, bearing in mind that they are still in the early stages of their developmental continuum, what they are feeling is quite predictable. I explain that their feelings are *so pre- dictable* that I have taken this into consideration when designing the school's integrated ITT/NQT Professional Studies calendar. The ration- ale of the programme is shown in Figure 5.3 opposite. The role of the mentor changes as the beginning teacher moves through the year and becomes more confident (see Furlong and Maynard, 1995).

My message to you as beginning teachers is not to become cynical, and not to lose sight of your early idealism or the value of using the humanist approach in the classroom. It is fair to say, however, that you may have to put some of your methods *on hold* until you feel that you have a classroom and behaviour management infrastructure firm- ly in place. When you feel you have got these pupils working in the way you want them to, then you can then gradually re-introduce the humanist approach. I place great emphasis on the importance of the establishment phase of the year, and of the need for teachers to

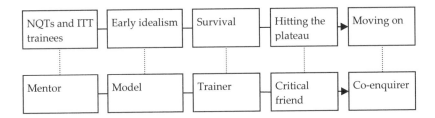

Figure 5.3: Developmental stages of NQTs and ITT trainees and the changing role of the mentor

outline their rules, routines and expectations strongly with the pupils (Dixie, 2003). Using the humanist approach on its own, without giving due concern to the needs of pupils for clear and secure boundaries, will simply not work. I like to feel that I adopt a humanist approach with my pupils. However, 'come rain or shine', at the start of each year, and with each new class, I spend about three quarters of an hour outlining my expectations to the pupils. I would strongly suggest that you do the same. Adopt a firm and assertive manner that shows the pupils that you really *mean business* and support this approach with firm and well-considered sanctions. You might like, for instance, to produce a 'Start the Year' presentation pack. For example, you could make copies of your rules, routines, expectations and sanctions that pupils could stick into their exercise books. These should be supported with illustrations which are designed to get your message across to the visual learners in your classes. Below is an example of my expectations to help pupils get it right.

- If the room is locked, line up *quietly* outside the room.
- Enter the room *quietly*, get your book and equipment out and work quietly on the starter tasks set for you.
- On entry to the classroom check whether you need to pick up resources from the back desk.
- Save your personal conversations with me until *I* am ready to talk to you.
- If you finish the set task, then stick any loose sheets into your book, remove old worksheets, underline titles and generally tidy your work up.

- At the end of the 3-2-1 countdown signal, stop talking and give me your full attention. You are to be silent when I am taking the register.
- Make sure your homework is recorded, completed and handed in on time.
- Treat the classroom with respect.
- At the end of the lesson, tuck your chairs in, pick up any litter off the floor, return your resources, stand behind your tables and wait until I give you permission to leave the room.

You are advised to make sure you constantly re-visit these rules and routines as you move through the year. An effective way of doing this is to give the pupils a true or false quiz. I have included below a few statements from one of my quizzes, 'How well do you know my rules and routines?', to serve as an example.

- I do not mind you being a few minutes late for my lessons.
- If the door is unlocked you are allowed to enter the room.
- You are expected to enter the room quietly.
- The beginning of the lesson is always a good time to have a personal conversation with me.
- You are allowed five late pieces of homework before you are put into detention.

It is also useful to have a series of PowerPoint slides designed to get across to the pupils the notion that teaching is very much a *deal* that requires give and take on both sides. As well as outlining what you expect from the pupils, you should make sure that they understand exactly what they can *expect from you* during the course of the year, for example:

- I will mark your books once a week.
- I will provide you with constructive feedback.
- I will be there to listen to you.
- I will help you to celebrate your success.

You can design a series of motivational posters and PowerPoint slides to inspire, motivate and increase the self-esteem of your pupils. I have again included a few examples below which are just some of the many motivational quotations I use in my 'Starting the Year' presentation in September. These are easily obtained from the Internet.

'Kites rise highest against the wind – not with it' (Sir Winston Churchill). I use this expression to explain to the pupils that I am there to celebrate their success but to also act as a critical friend.

'Warm bath – cold shower' Always celebrate success but ensure you challenge youngsters constantly. Show them how to move on.

You will note that with the approach described above, there is a strong emphasis on using classroom and behaviour management strategies to set up teacher expectations in lessons. You may remember from reading Chapter 1 that I refer to this as a teacher's technical competence. However, you will also note that I have introduced a number of humanist elements into the presentation, that is, the idea of building up good teacher/pupil relationships; the notion that both parties have responsibilities in the learning equation; the importance of pupil self-esteem and self-expectation. I generally find that, providing the initial part of the presentation is carried out in an assertive and businesslike fashion, I am usually successful in establishing a meaningful classroom ethos for the rest of the year. However, the important thing to remember is that if you want to maintain this positive ethos in your classroom, you have to remind your pupils constantly of your rules, routines and expectations. Make no bones about it, failure to do so *will* result in a breakdown in relationships with your pupils.

Getting pupils more involved

Up to this point, we have discussed the merits of using a dual strategy in managing your classes for effective learning – using clearly thought out behaviour management plans whilst at the same time combining this with a humanistic approach. One essential ingredient which is of the utmost importance in producing good pupil/teacher relationships, and good learning scenarios, relates to the degree of *ownership* pupils have of the learning process.

My experiences of interviewing pupils about their teachers have shown me that the most popular teachers are those who allow pupils to have their say and to make a positive contribution to lessons. It is fair to say, however, that in the past, most classrooms were dominated by teachers talking, with few opportunities for pupils to contribute verbally to lessons. Barnes (1979), cited in Kyriacou (2001), described how, even in situations where teachers did allow pupils to contribute verbally to lessons, these contributions were channelled along predetermined lines. The dominant message to pupils seemed to be that any response that did not fit closely enough with the teacher's requirements, would be rejected as being irrelevant. You will appreciate the net result of this. Pupils simply tapered their responses to suit the narrow remit of the question being asked. In other words, they simply had to guess what the teacher was thinking. I am sure you will agree that this is a far cry from the intellectual needs of pupils to think in a lateral and creative way. As we have already seen, much of the reluctance to allow pupils to explore their own views and ideas is often down to the insecurity and low-esteem of the teachers themselves. You, as beginning teachers, might like to consider where you stand on this issue. In an effort to gain control over proceedings in your classes, do you tend to restrict the level of verbal input into your lessons? Do you feel ready to let go yet? I have included a few suggestions that might help you to give your pupils greater ownership of their lessons.

- Give your pupils the rationale behind your need for them to respond to your questions. Ask them to focus on the questions being asked, to formulate the necessary language required to respond, to take a risk and put their hand up in lessons. Stress the fact that doing this is not just about being a 'boff'! As you can see from Figure 5.4, it is important to get this message across to your pupils in a visual manner. See Dixie (2003) to find out more on this strategy.

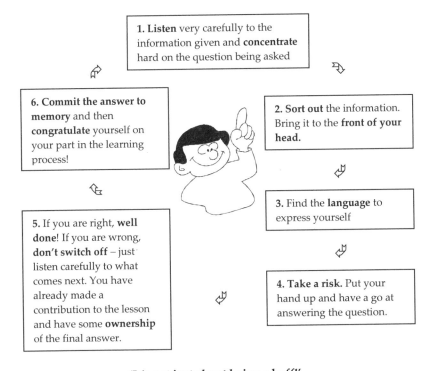

'It's not just about being a boff!'

Reproduced from Dixie, *Managing Your Classroom*, 2003, by permission of Continuum International Publishing Group Ltd, The Tower Building, 11 York Road, London SE1 7NX, UK

Figure 5.4: Getting the climate right for question and answer sessions

- Get your pupils to ask the questions. Start off the lesson by displaying some stimulus material and ask the pupils to come up with as many exploratory questions as possible. In other words, ask them what they want to know about the topic. I have found that giving the pupils greater ownership of a topic dramatically increases their participation and motivation, and most certainly strengthens the bond between myself and the class.

- There is no better way to learn about something than having to teach it to somebody else! Divide a topic area up into discrete areas and ask your pupils to prepare presentations. By building in a system of peer-assessment, you will introduce a degree of status to the activity and the pupils are more likely to take the activity seriously. My experiences show that the pupils enjoy learning in this manner. They readily admit that the additional pressure of having to get things right means that they are more likely to take the material on board.

- Provide plenty of opportunities for paired and group work activities, but make sure that your pupils work *together* rather than in a parallel fashion.

- Come up with a set of negotiated rules for group work. Doing this will help the pupils to think responsibly about the way in which they work and, will again, give them greater owner- ship of the lesson. If pupils are to gain maximum benefit from the group work process, it is absolutely vital that you allow them the opportunity to discuss the rationale behind these rules. In Figure 5.5 I have laid out a few examples from a list of group work rules I negotiated with pupils in my classes.

- Set up a 'buddy' mentoring system whereby pupils offer gui- dance and advice to each other.

- Accept the value of each pupil's contribution. Give credence and respectability to those lateral thinkers in the class who come up with responses that might not be seen as main- stream.

- Allow more 'Wait Time' (Zimpher and Howey, 1987), cited in Dixie (2003) when asking questions. Giving pupils that extra few seconds or so to respond will dramatically increase the number of voluntary responses offered in class discussions and question/answer sessions.

Rules	Rationale
You should work *together* as a group. This means you will have to plan your work *together*. Remember, a chain is only as strong as its weakest link.	By doing this you will be able to share ideas and learn from each other. You will also be able to improve your inter-personal skills.
You need to appoint a group co-ordinator. This should be someone who is well-organised, good with people and someone who can motivate the group to get the work done properly.	Making the right decision here rather than simply choosing your friend will help all of you in the group to succeed and to realise your potential.
Find out about other people's preferred learning styles. Work to people's strengths.	Doing this will allow people in the group to show what they can do and to produce a balanced presentation.
Make sure you communicate effectively with other people in the group. Swap e-mail addresses, telephone numbers etc.	Doing this will mean that time will not be wasted and that you will be able to work efficiently as a group.

Figure 5.5: Group work rules

One of the most important aspects of classroom interaction relates to the choice of words and tone of voice used by teachers in their dealings with pupils. Young people are extremely sensitive to the slightest critical inflexion in voice tone and/or use of language that appears to be a personal attack on them. Many of our pupils will be at a stage in their lives where self-esteem is low and where they may feel particularly vulnerable in front of their peers. It is imperative, therefore, that we choose our words and tone of voice very carefully. This is particularly important when we are reprimanding misbehaviour, or when we are reacting to pupils' responses in class discussions or question/ answer sessions. As we have seen in Chapter 3, difficult as this is, it is absolutely vital that when you admonish pupils, you focus your attention on the inappropriate nature of their behaviour rather than on them as individuals. Do not insult pupils, *and* make it clear that there are no personal grudges behind the messages you are issuing. It is also absolutely essential that you ask the pupil to accompany you out of the classroom so that you do not embarrass them in front to their peers. I have included a brief example of a typical conversation I might have with a youngster who has over-stepped the mark in one of my classes. 'Would you mind if I had a brief word with you outside the classroom please, Robert?' (This would be said in an assertive but polite tone of voice before I turn away and walk towards the classroom door in an expectant fashion.) When we are both outside the classroom, I ask Robert to move away from the door so that we cannot be overheard by the other pupils inside the room. Then in a firm but non-aggressive tone of voice, I would say something like this:

> 'Things are not going too well today, are they Robert – is there any particular reason for this?'
>
> 'No, sir,' Robert grunts.
>
> 'Robert, before I say anything else to you, you need to know that this is not a personal attack on you. You're a nice lad but this behaviour seems out of character to me and is not acceptable. Robert, you need to know that you are good at this subject and that you have a lot to offer in lessons. I know you are honest enough to appreciate the fact that your behaviour is not only stopping you from learning, but that it is also having a bad effect on the others in the class. Would you agree that this is a fair comment?'
>
> 'Yes, sir, sorry sir.'

You will notice that in this very short dialogue there are a lot of positive messages. First, Robert knows that it is the inappropriateness of his behaviour, and not him personally, I am criticising. Second, by using the words 'I know you are honest enough to appreciate', I am setting up positive expectations of Robert as a human being. I usually find that this low key approach is often enough to diffuse difficult situations and get the pupil back to work.

Always try to be positive when pupils give incorrect or inappropriate answers in class and try to find a way of using their responses to take the discussion further. Never put a pupil down for a wrong answer! If you do, they will remember this for a very long time and will be highly unlikely to volunteer a contribution again.

A great deal of sociological research has been carried out into the effect of labelling of pupils by teachers. My role as a sociology teacher has heightened my awareness of this issue of labelling and the works of Rist (1970) and Keddie (1976) have influenced my teaching greatly over the past ten years or so. So, what exactly is labelling? It is the way in which pupils are encouraged and/or taught to see themselves by their teachers. As we have already seen, not all labelling is a bad thing; positive labelling can create self-belief in pupils and really play a part in motivating them to succeed both academically and socially. However, we must all be very careful about labelling pupils in a negative way. This is often done in an overt way by referring to pupils as nasty, evil, thick, trouble-makers etc. I am not exaggerating here – in my role as professional development tutor I have to listen to some particularly vitriolic descriptions of pupils made by a few beginning teachers, who are struggling to get to grips with some particularly challenging classes. 'I hate taking 9M2! They simply don't want to know. They are all just a bunch of trouble-makers. I'll be glad to see the back of them at the end of the year.' These teachers have failed to grasp two things; first, they are taking up a defensive stance and are failing to confront their own practice; second, they are failing to see that children usually live up to the expectations placed upon them. When teachers label children, it is not surprising that these youngsters live up to these expectations. In building a positive climate we should create an atmosphere where our first assumption should be one of success, respect and high self-esteem.

Negative labelling can, of course, occur in a more subtle form than in some of the examples described above. Ignoring specific pupils during class discussions and question/answer sessions, using negative body language towards pupils can all convey distaste or lack of expectations. The point I am making here is that if the pupils receive these negative messages enough times, they will begin to believe and assimilate them. One of the early founders of the Interactionist School of Sociology, Charles Cooley, developed the concept of the 'looking glass image' (1902) to explain the effects of labelling. The basis of his theory was that the actions of a person will very much depend upon that person's interpretation of the way they are perceived. For this reason, many interactionists place particular emphasis on the idea of 'self'. They suggest that individuals develop an image or self-concept and that this has an important influence on their actions. A pupil's self-concept depends on the reactions of others towards him or her: hence the term 'looking-glass image'. In short, we tend to act in terms of our self-image. So, if pupils are constantly defined as lazy, arrogant

and rude they will tend to see themselves in this light and act accordingly. Surely it cannot be as simple as that! Well, my experience tells me it is. I am suggesting that you take a measured look at the teaching staff in your school, that you identify those teachers who experience poor relationships with their pupils, and then see whether I am right or not. To me, the following piece of writing sums it up superbly.

> If children live with criticism, they learn to condemn.
> If children live with hostility, they learn to fight.
> If children live with ridicule, they learn to be shy.
> If children live with tolerance, they learn to be patient.
> If children live with encouragement, they learn confidence.
> If children live with praise, they learn to appreciate.
> If children live with fairness, they learn justice.
> If children live with security, they learn to have faith.
> If children live with approval, they learn to like themselves.
> If children live with acceptance and friendship, they learn to find love in the world. (Author unknown)

Now I know that, as beginning teachers, you will be unable to do anything about what I call 'structural labelling' – that is where the organisation of the school sends out strong messages to pupils about their place in the institution's hierarchy. You are not in control of the way in which your school groups its pupils, but you are in a position to control what goes on in your classroom. You must become aware of how much power you hold over the pupils through your experience and your superior use of language. In the words of Rogers (1998), you need to practise developing a 'positive verbal style'.

There is no doubt in my mind whatsoever, that if you give considered thought to how you want the physical, social and emotional climate of your classroom to be, you can create a scenario that raises and maintains high pupil self-esteem. In order to achieve this you need to do a number of things:

- make the focus and objectives for the learning transparent;
- provide opportunities for pupils of all abilities to feel they have accomplished something;
- provide opportunities for social interaction between pupils;
- make encouragement and praise task-specific and not general in nature;
- give overt and equal status to pupils with all types of intelligences;
- treat your pupils with respect and dignity;
- admit your mistakes to your pupils.

Ask any teacher and they will tell you that the worst thing about the job is marking. It is important to realise, however, that marking pupils' work is not just about assessment! Whenever you take a set of exercise books home to mark, or settle down to mark a batch of test papers, think of this as an opportunity not only to develop the learning potential of your pupils, but also as a means of developing your relationships with them. We all know that feedback to pupils should be formative in nature, providing them with advice and guidance about how to move on academically, setting them realistic targets and generally using the assessed assignment as a learning tool. However, it is important not to underestimate the power of your summative written comments as a tool for establishing and developing your relationships with your pupils. Using words such as 'rubbish', 'useless', etc. will serve absolutely no purpose either in getting the youngster back on track, or in helping to develop good working relationships with them in the future. Take as many opportunities as possible to praise your pupils. I always try to support my formative assessment comments with personalised comments such as 'You have come so far over the past year' or 'You should be really proud of your efforts here' or 'Tremendous effort here'.

I strongly advise that you not only make use of the school's credit system, but that you develop your own system for rewarding pupils. Quite honestly, the way I see it, the more daft the system the better it is. In my classes if pupils produce a piece of good work they receive an 'Oven Glove Award' stamp which I had made up at a local printer. The notion behind this is that their work is so 'hot' that I have had to put on an oven glove to mark it! When the pupils receive six stamps, they are then eligible for a raffle ticket which could win them a CD voucher at the end of each term. In situations where pupils do something exceptional, or where they make a consistently high effort over a long period of time, I send one of my specially designed postcards home as a way of informing their parents.

Although, I am often referred to as 'sad' by my pupils, I know that they value this recognition of their efforts more than the formal reward system. Whichever method you choose, you really must make sure you utilise some form of reward system in your lessons. Failure to do so will generally result in a lack of motivation, poor behaviour and low work rate. All of this will contribute towards a break-down in relationships with your pupils.

Strangely enough one of the best ways of striking up good working relationships with pupils is through their parents. This can be done either through the medium of the parents consultation sessions, making personal telephone calls home and/or through the school's reporting system. I know how many members of staff baulk at the thought of spending yet another three to four hours at parents consultation evenings after a hard day's work at school. In my opinion, however, using these sessions creatively and positively can be one of the biggest potential investments you can make in a child. A successful consultation with parents can play a major part in helping to turn the youngster around in terms of their academic work and/or as far as their relationship with you is concerned. My advice to any young teacher attending parents' evenings would be to take the opportunity of starting off the session by praising the child or by talking about the pupil's good qualities, even if the child is being difficult or not really achieving his or her full potential. I know what the reaction of some teachers would be to this – 'but there is nothing redeemable about Gary' or 'Quite honestly, I feel that Sharon is simply a pain in the backside. When she's not there I breathe a sigh of relief. I cannot think of anything nice to say about her'. I have actually heard teachers say that they hate some of their pupils. As far as I am concerned, remarks such as these tell me more about the teacher than they do about the pupils. Of course some of these pupils *are* difficult. Of course, life would be a lot easier if they were not in school, but the truth is that you are never going to get them to change their ways unless you show you have recognised their strengths and qualities. Showing warmth and a positive attitude towards their children can make a real impression on parents, and these messages are almost certainly likely to be cascaded directly to the child when they get home.

As far as I am concerned, the same principles apply to writing of reports. I am extremely critical of the 'cut and paste' descriptor level style reports used by many schools to report progress today. In the past, I have been told not to 'over personalise' my reports but to focus on giving information about the child's current state of learning as measured by a formal set of criteria. Of course this is important, but unless I recognise the pupil as an individual, they are highly unlikely to make any progress in my lessons.

So what happens when a youngster is not doing the business in lessons? What happens if they are under-achieving? Do you try to soften the blow? Do you lie? No, of course not. What you should do is to make a real effort to get to know the whole child. Talk to the youngster before you write the report, get their perspective on the issue and make it clear in your reports that you like the pupils concerned, and that you want to work with them to help them realise their potential. Just using a simple phrase such as: 'As much as I like Joe, it is fair to say that ...' at the beginning of the report gets the message over to Joe that the suggestions you are going to make have been made with his best interests at heart. That is all very well when you *do* actually like the pupil concerned, but what on earth do you write when you really *do not* like the youngster? You must never feel guilty about not liking a pupil – we cannot like everybody we meet. Very often it is really difficult to like someone who has been unco-operative, who has sworn at you or who has generally made your life hell. It is important, however, that the general tenet of your report should demonstrate respect for the pupil concerned. In other words, you should again be focusing your attentions on the inappropriate nature of the pupil's actions and not using condemnatory language to show your dislike for them.

Teaching, as you have probably found out, is not an exact science. You will already have received a catalogue of advice from a whole range of people throughout your career. Some of this guidance will have been useful, whilst other contributions may have turned out to be inappropriate. All I have tried to do in this chapter is to furnish you with a number of things that have worked for me and that have help-ed to develop my relationships with my pupils. Obviously, I believe my guiding principles to be worth considering, but the specific detail of how you realise these principles is down to you. Although I feel that it is absolutely imperative you set up a positive ethos in your classroom, you must be true to yourself and you must do so in a style that is sympathetic to your own personality traits. If you adopt these principles then I see no reason why you should not enjoy successful relationships with the pupils in your classes. It is, however, very im-portant for me to say that the setting up of a positive classroom infra-structure is not, on its own, the panacea to solving all relationship problems with your pupils. There will still be a number of pupils for whom this approach will not work and who continue to be difficult and disrupt the learning of others. The following chapter explores ways in which you can establish and maintain good relations with these challenging youngsters, and goes on to explain how you can minimise disruption in your lessons.

Chapter 6

Understanding and
Supporting Challenging Pupils

It may be consoling for you to know that even good teachers have some discipline problems. Teachers who say they never experience behavioural problems in their classes are at best deluding themselves and at worst simply lying. I suspect that many of you would not expect me, as a teacher of long-standing experience, to have behavioural problems with my pupils. This is an unrealistic expectation to hold! Of course, I do everything I can to set up an infrastructure for good discipline in my classes, but teaching is not a static process and pupils are not like robots responding to a programming system. Despite the best planning, things can go wrong. There have been many occasions during my long career where, because of the actions of a few challenging pupils, my behaviour management plans have been shot to pieces. I have had to apply alternative strategies to deal effectively with some extremely tricky situations.

Schools vary greatly in their responses to disruptive pupils. Some schools have on-site behavioural units where youngsters may be sent for a cooling-off period; though in some areas, however, disruptive pupils spend time at off-site units which are designed to reduce the effects of challenging behaviour in the classroom. There are also marked differences in attitude in the approaches made by schools towards their disruptive pupils' behaviour. Some schools take a sympathetic counselling approach towards this anti-social behaviour, whilst others are far more robust in their responses, but it is not within the remit of this publication to explore the wider structural strategies for dealing with indiscipline in schools. The fundamental purpose of this chapter is to explore the agenda of disruptive pupils and to offer some strategies to help you deal effectively with these youngsters in your lessons.

To become successful in dealing with challenging pupils, you need to be fully aware of the interactive nature of teaching; a process that requires an ever-changing system of exchange and negotiation between you and your pupils. It is important for you to remember that it is not simply a case of you employing the 'jug and mug' principle, with the children being the empty receptacles into which you simply pour a healthy portion of knowledge. No longer should the pupils be considered as the passive recipients of the teacher's subject expertise. It is important for all of us to remember that pupils bring their own socially constructed agenda into the classroom. These agenda have been formed through their experiences both at home and at school and manifest themselves in the idiosyncrasies, expectations, aspirations and intentions brought into your classroom. It is, therefore, to be expected that at some point during the working day, even the most effective and skilful of teachers will experience a *conflict of interest* between the values of the school and those of some youngsters in their classes. It is your role as a teacher to reduce the number of situations that could conflict with the ultimate aim of the lesson – that of producing an effective learning scenario for pupils.

So, what exactly constitutes disruptive behaviour? All teachers experience some relatively minor low-level disruption in their classes from time to time. Indeed, research shows that this type of misbehaviour is far more common than the more serious breaches of discipline that occur during the year (Dixie 2003; Wragg, 1984). An effective behaviour management plan will usually help to eradicate these minor pupil indiscretions. However, the type of scenario we must concern ourselves with in this chapter is where the behaviour of a pupil

- seriously undermines the teacher's ability to establish and maintain effective learning scenarios; and/or
- threatens the safety of the teacher or other pupils in the class.

There is no doubt that this type of behaviour is on the increase in our schools today and that it is of real concern to teachers across the

United Kingdom. A major survey involving more than 2,500 teachers in thirteen local education authorities across England and Wales was carried out by the National Union of Teachers in 2001. This survey revealed that more than 80 per cent of teachers in schools of all types – in rural, urban and inner city areas – said that pupil behaviour had deteriorated during their time in teaching. Only 10 per cent said there had been little or no deterioration. The report went on to say that even some pupils in nursery schools displayed high levels of unacceptable behaviour. Examples included incidents that involved children using offensive language, making abusive and insulting comments, and threatening teachers. Commenting on the results of the survey, Doug McAvoy, NUT General Secretary, said:

> This survey shows an unacceptable level of physical and verbal aggression between pupils, and directed at teachers. Many of the comments point to teachers seeing this behaviour as the final straw in causing them to leave teaching even though they love it.

I must make it clear that I have not cited this information in order to alarm you or to initiate any kind of moral panic. I am convinced that, despite these worrying trends, most pupil indiscipline can be eradicated through the use of good classroom management ploys and by using a humanistic approach towards teaching, as described and discussed in Chapter 5.

So, what exactly constitutes seriously disruptive behaviour? I think that if you asked most teachers to describe the characteristics of pupils who seriously disrupt their lessons, they would easily be able to come up with a list of common inappropriate and anti-social behaviour. My newly qualified teachers and teacher trainees produced the following list during one of my behavioural management sessions:

- making an attention-seeking entry into the classroom;
- constantly and persistently shouting out;
- making inappropriate comments;
- refusing to do any work;
- throwing things across the classroom;
- hitting or goading other pupils;
- being rude and aggressive;
- disobeying and challenging the authority of the teacher.

Unfortunately, very often these disruptive pupils display a combination of these behaviours. Unless the individual class teacher can stem the tide, a cumulative effect tends to occur, with a minor incident that perhaps finally precipitates the school's decision to exclude the pupil. Mitchell (1996), whose research findings mirrored most of the behaviours shown above, classified the most frequently precipitating incidents into five categories:

- physical abuse, including assaults on children, teachers and other adults;
- verbal abuse, including insolence, swearing and disobedience to staff, and abusive behaviour to other pupils;
- disruption, including disruption in lessons, refusal to accept punishments, breaking contracts, and misbehaviour that disrupts the smooth running of the school;
- criminal behaviour, including drug-related activities, vandalism and theft;
- truancy; other attendance problems, including absconding.

It is likely that many of you recognise these anti-social behaviours in some form or another amongst the pupils in some of your classes. It is also highly likely that many of these behaviours have underlying and interrelated causes that may not lie within the realms of the school, or within the remit of the ordinary subject teacher. Sociologists refer to these causes as 'outside-school explanations for differential motivation and achievement'. These outside-school explanations include factors such as child-rearing practices, the physical conditions of the home environment, the stability of family relationships and the cultural attitudes of parents towards education. Whilst it is vital that you have an understanding of the role of these factors in shaping the lives of your pupils, it is important for you to remember that there are limitations to what you can do personally to redress these issues in the early stages of your teaching career. It is, therefore, not within the remit of this chapter to explore the argument about whether schools should or should not be expected to compensate for society. Any guidance or advice offered will be restricted to what you as subject teachers or form tutors can reasonably be expected to do to minimise instances of disruptive behaviour in your classes. Having said all this, do not underestimate the importance of a friendly and enquiring word about 'how things are going at home'. As you will see later in the chapter, taking the time to talk through issues with challenging pupils can work wonders for your relationships with them in the classroom. However, be realistic and do not expect to be able to put these problems right entirely on your own.

We have seen in Chapter 3 how important it is for a teacher to be *reflective*. No matter how threatening the situation might seem, I would advise you to look inward at what you are doing in the class-room, before you resort to employing heavy-handed sanctions. 'Com-ing the heavy', without fully evaluating whether you have done your bit to provide a stimulating and sympathetic learning scenario, will only serve to cause hostility and resentment amongst your pupils. A study by Marsh *et al.* (1978) involving interviewing pupils labelled as 'disruptive', revealed some very interesting perspectives. Many of the pupils interviewed felt provoked into misbehaving and talked about the teacher insulting them and being responsible for them losing their dignity and self-esteem in front of their peers. Marsh *et al.* classified these behaviours into four categories:

- teachers who were boring;
- teachers who could not teach;
- teachers whose discipline was weak;
- teachers who made unfair comparisons.

As far as these pupils were concerned their behaviour was justi-fied. They were only *fighting back* in a situation where they had felt under threat. It needs to be said that whilst these perceptions continue to exist, then quite simply, lessons will continue to be disrupted and conflict will inevitably occur. As highlighted in Chapter 4, it is impor-tant for you as beginning teachers to ascertain the perceptions of your pupils about the way things are going in your lessons. As we also discussed earlier, giving your pupils some ownership of the lessons will go a long way to reducing this conflict and help to make them feel part of the learning process.

You will already be aware that many behavioural problems prob-ably occur in classrooms because of the increasing number of pupils with special educational needs. It is important to remember that a great deal of misbehaviour occurs simply because these pupils do not understand the work that has been set for them. The youngster is often in a no-win situation here. If he or she tries to do the work, they are likely to meet with frustration and failure, and then subsequently incur the wrath of the teacher. If the pupil opts out of doing the work, he or she is likely to become bored and start to distract other pupils around them. Again, this is likely to incur the teacher's displeasure. It is vital that you, as teachers, take a step back and try to show some empathy for these youngsters. I do not know what your science or mathematics background is like, but mine is virtually non-existent. Whenever I start to get exasperated with pupils who simply cannot understand the work, I try to reproduce the following imaginary but, nevertheless, nightmare scenario.

I am sitting in a lecture hall listening to one of the world's most eminent scientists give a lecture on Einstein's Theory of Relativity. I am starting to panic because my tutor has asked me to take notes and to use these to make a verbal presentation to the seminar group when next we meet. I haven't got a clue as to what the professor is talking about! I look around me and notice all my friends nodding in the right places and taking reams of copious notes. My heart starts to beat faster and I break out in a cold sweat at the thought of my task. The only way out of this situation is for me to pretend I don't care. I screw up my notepaper and fling it surreptitiously at my friend sitting to my left. He gives me a disapproving sideways look. I put my hand to my mouth, give a fake yawn, raise my eyebrows in mock boredom and then walk out of the lecture hall in *disgust* thinking about all the excuses I can offer for not being able to give this feedback session.

My advice is for you to put yourself in the position of those pupils who find much of their schoolwork challenging and stressful. Try to re-create situations where *you* have found things difficult and where pressure to succeed has been placed unfairly upon *you*. By doing this, you will get an understanding of what many of these youngsters are going through. It will also help you to find the right verbal and body language to deal sympathetically with their difficulties. In addition to this, you need to make it your business to find out about some of the more common special educational needs (SEN) conditions such as ADHD, autism and dyslexia. You need to use this information to cater for these pupils in your lessons. Speak to your special educational needs co-ordinator (SENCO), and read up about these conditions and try to find out as much as you can about the specific needs of the individuals in your classes. You should also be aware that when seriously disruptive pupils are referred to the educational psychologist, they are assessed for either behavioural or emotional disorders. The former relates to such things as anti-social behaviour, truancy, stealing, and violence towards others, whilst the latter relates to such emotional behaviours as anxieties, depression, self-harm, withdrawal, and problems in establishing and maintaining relationships.

If your pupils are displaying any of the symptoms described above, check your records to see if they have been identified as being on the special needs register. If they are not on this register, then have a word with your head of department or SENCO. These youngsters might have slipped through the net. Providing you do this, and providing that you have acted positively upon the advice offered above, as beginning teachers, you cannot be expected to do more.

Pre-empting difficult behaviour

Okay, so you have implemented all the advice and guidance about setting up a positive classroom ethos as offered in Chapter 5, but there are still a number of pupils whose behaviour you are finding difficult to deal with. So what do you do?

As with your behaviour/classroom management plan, there are a number of things you can do to prevent conflict and to avoid your lessons being seriously disrupted by these challenging youngsters.

- You need to get to know what makes these pupils tick. Read all their records, talk to these youngsters, talk to their form tutors, to their heads of year and, if you feel able to, find out from their parents what they are like at home. By doing this, you will be able to get a *feeling* for the pupils concerned.
- Even if you have had trouble with these youngsters, go out of your way to be friendly to them when you see them around the school. Ask them how they are. Ask them what they did over the weekend – just be friendly to them. Often the mere act of using a pupil's name and talking to them as *real* people, is akin to making psychological contracts with them (Dixie, 2003). Even if they are looking for trouble, pupils find it more difficult to misbehave when, perhaps in the corridor half an hour earlier, you were asking how their football match went over the weekend.
- Find a moment to talk formally with these individual pupils. Notice that I said talk *with* and not *to*. Often challenging and disruptive pupils have study periods allocated to them when they have been excluded from some of their classes. If your non-contact periods coincide with any of these, use this time to find out about these pupils. I can almost hear you say – 'I am too busy to do this'. My response is simple – if you do not make the effort to do this, you will end up more stressed and you will spend far more time sorting out discipline problems.
- Involve yourself in extra curricular activities such as sport, drama, school clubs, school trips, and so forth. Find common interests with your pupils. (Some of the biggest rogues in my school belong to the school football team. Football is a particular passion of mine and often forms the focal point of much discussion between the rogues and myself.) Take time to notice and comment upon qualities displayed by these pupils in their various activities. 'You're a really good team player, Nathan!' 'You showed real strength of character today, Gary!' 'You've got your team really playing well for each other, Shelly!' 'You're a born leader, Michael!'
- Observing the body language and facial expressions of these youngsters before they enter the classroom can really help to inform the way you interact with them in your lessons. Just making a reflective statement about the way the pupil looks

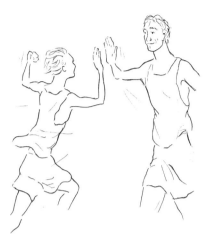

conveys care and concern to them and can act as a calming effect on the situation. You could say something like: 'You don't look very happy today, Aaron. Things not going well? Hang on here a minute, I'll get the rest of the class in and settled and we can have a brief chat.' Although you are often not in a position to sort the problem out for the youngster, just showing that you care enough to ask them how they are feeling is sometimes enough to get that pupil to behave in your class, simply out of loyalty to you. If any issues crop up that you do not feel confident in dealing with, tell the pupil you will do your best to find someone who can help them.

- Establishing the use of a private signal between the pupil and myself is something that works for me. For example, when the pupil makes a letter 'T' for 'time-out' with their fingers, it signifies that he or she needs a brief cooling-off period outside the classroom. The knowledge that they have an escape clause in the lesson acts as a form of security, enough to keep them working in the classroom on their assigned task.

- If the youngster needs to leave the room, do not let him or her wander in the corridor. Arrange for a safe and secure place. Perhaps a colleague could supervise in an office or an empty classroom. However, it is absolutely vital that your colleague is supportive of your methods and that he or she does not immediately start to launch into the pupil about the inappropriateness of his or her behaviour.

- You could tell the pupil that you need their help, for example asking them to help another youngster in the room with their work. Doing this gives off two messages: first, that you trust them, and second, that they have something to offer and are useful. Remember that raising self-esteem is vital for these youngsters.

- Knowing your pupils well will enable you to provide appropriate materials and topics that interest them. You could ask some of your more challenging pupils to launch the lesson by talking about specific issues, or by bringing in items or artefacts which relate to the topics under study. Again, being the 'expert' can often do wonders for pupil self-esteem as well as doing a great deal to improve your relationships with these.

- Choosing these youngsters for leadership roles often works in raising their self-esteem. You could, for example, make them captains of class quiz teams.

- Go with the flow. Do not try to do battle for the conformist middle classes. Do not be too judgemental and try to accept that you will never be able to stop these youngsters totally from doing what is considered by most, to be socially unacceptable. Be realistic and accept that you will not be able to alter what has taken them over a decade to learn outside school. Just focus your attention on small-scale improvements in their behaviour and continue to make the point that the negative behaviour being exhibited is unacceptable in your lessons.

- The physical size of pupils can often appear to be a problem. It is important to remember that even the biggest and most truculent of youths, are frequently insecure and vulnerable on the inside. Do not, therefore, under any circumstance, use sarcasm to belittle the pupil or as a means of gaining control of a situation.

- If all these methods fail, do not beat yourself up. It can take a long time to build up a reputation amongst the school population for fair play and honesty, and is bound to include a number of failures on the way. Just let the pupils know you care and refer the issue to a senior and respected colleague.

Understanding the needs of the adolescent

There is a point when you are going to have to go beyond being pragmatic and when you are going to need to try to get under the skin of your difficult pupils in order to try to understand them fully. With most pupils, an understanding of what it is like to be young, is usually enough to get you through the day. However, I do feel that in extreme cases the need to understand adolescent behaviour is heightened. So, what exactly is an adolescent and what constitutes typical adolescent behaviour? Bearing in mind that, in most cultures, a youngster of 14 or 15 years of age would normally have joined the adult world, the following observation of adolescence seems be quite apposite.

> Adolescence is where evolution says you're a grown-up but where a grown-up says you're a child. (Source unknown)

Although I am no psychologist, I feel that my experience and my background reading allow me to offer a list of features which are generally associated with adolescence. These are:

- moodiness and mood swings;
- argumentativeness;
- a tendency to challenge authority;
- hyper-sensitivity to criticism;

- a sense of isolation and persecution;
- unnecessary risk-taking;
- confused identity;
- being hyper-critical of others;
- fluctuating self-esteem;
- difficulties in making sense of the world, and establishing own values and beliefs;
- preoccupation with image;
- obsession with sex and relationships;
- conflicting needs that waiver between wanting to be independent and wanting to belong.

The following observation made by the psychologist Louise Kaplan (1984) sums up the uncertain world in which the adolescence lives.

> Adolescence represents an inner emotional upheaval, a struggle between eternal human wish to cling on to the past and the equally powerful wish to get on with the future.

Let's face it, this degree of emotional upheaval and stress is hard enough to bear for the most stable of people, let alone for youngsters who may come from emotionally and physically disadvantaged backgrounds.

Effective relationships with all pupils, but particularly with challenging individuals, must come from our knowledge of what the needs of human beings are. A teacher, therefore, needs to know about the 'human givens'. So, what exactly are the human givens?

Human givens are what we are born with. They are our genetic endowment – our physical and emotional needs that have been programmed into us throughout the course of history. Human givens also include the resources with which nature has provided us to help us meet those needs.

Teachers who show an empathic understanding for the human givens of young people, are more likely to establish and maintain good working relationships with their pupils. Whether you possess a formal understanding of these needs, or whether you do this intuitively, is irrelevant. What is important is that you actually demonstrate your understanding of the needs of your pupils and that you do everything you can to furnish them with the resources to meet these needs. Take a look at the following lists of emotional needs and resources and ask yourself what you do both in and out of the classroom to support your pupils.

Emotional needs
- security – stable family life, safe living environment;
- being able to make autonomous decisions;
- having a sense of belonging in the community;
- the need to be noticed and to receive attention;
- the need for human attachment through friendship, love and intimacy, and emotional attachment to others;
- the need for status and self-esteem;
- the need to understand the world in which they live.

Resources
- long-term memory;
- curiosity and imagination – to help solve problems;
- the ability to understand the world and other people through story and metaphor;
- the ability to be reflective, objective and self-aware;
- the ability to empathize with others;
- a rational objective mind that can side-skip emotions and solve problems;
- an imagination that can show a different world.

As teachers we need to know a number of things. Many young people have problems because their physical and emotional needs are not being met in their lives. Whereas it is not possible for you, as beginning teachers, to compensate for the deficient home background of these youngsters, there are things which you can do to help your pupils to build up a set of resources that will help them to cope with challenging situations. Here are some suggestions:

- provide opportunities in your classes for rational thinking and for solving social problems. You could set up problem-solving group work to explore specific social dilemmas relating to such issues as divorce, relationships and poverty;
- use fiction and non-fiction material to demonstrate alternative ways of seeing the world, and as a means of encouraging empathy for the lives of others;
- encourage discussion groups to explore current social issues;
- encourage the use of a reflective journal by pupils;
- encourage pupils to take responsibility for their own actions.

We should also be aware that the mind and body are inextricably intertwined and that the emotional brain, when highly aroused, is likely to inhibit thought and objectivity. Hopefully, you will now begin to see the need to calm youngsters down before they start to behave inappropriately and do something they might later regret.

Producing behaviour management plans

I described in Chapter 3 and Chapter 5 the importance of establishing a classroom infrastructure sympathetic to producing good discipline and successful learning scenarios. I have also written at length about the need for teachers to use the appropriate 'language of correction' (Rogers, 1998) when dealing with the disruptive behaviour of classes or individuals. In this chapter, I have taken things a stage further and attempted to focus your attention on those children whose behaviour and attitudes seem to step beyond this level of planning. We have explored reasons why some of these children become difficult at school, and I have suggested a number of general strategies you might use to improve your working relationships with these youngsters. What happens, however, when you feel you have tried everything and yet nothing seems to have worked?

Picture this scenario. In your lesson you have got a couple of pupils who are, yet again, being particularly difficult. With ever in-creasing volume, you hear yourself saying the same things over and over again. 'How many times have I told you ...', 'Do I have to keep telling you ...', 'Will you please stop ...' The question that needs to be asked is whether you feel these tactics are successful in helping you to modify the behaviour of these youngsters. It is highly likely that these strategies are not working. So, where do you go from here? This is where a behaviour management plan comes in. This consists of an agreed strategy between the teacher and the individual whose be-haviour needs modifying in some way. There are also different types of plan. Some can be formal written documents that involve parents and other staff, whilst others can take the form of a personal verbal contract between teacher and pupil. The notion behind a behaviour management plan is that the teacher and pupil negotiate short and/or long-term targets for the pupil to help him or her to realise these goals. It is important to remember that it is this negotiation process that is *so* vital to the success of the plan. If things have got particularly bad, you may have reached the point where your relationship with a specific pupil has all but broken down. If this is the case, it will be necessary to bring in a third party, perhaps the pupil's form tutor, to broker the deal. See this process as a *strength*, not as a *weakness*!

The rationale behind behaviour management plans is the funda-mental belief that children can be helped to

- recognise and understand the reasons for their behaviours;
- improve their problem-solving skills;
- explore choices in behavioural responses;
- explore and accept the consequences of their actions.

It is important in the initial phases of designing your behaviour management plan that you take a realistic attitude about what can be achieved, and that you are not too ambitious. Bearing in mind that many of these youngsters already see themselves as failures, it is vital to build in a high degree of success in the early part of the plan. What I have done below is to offer you a suggested route through a plan from its inception right through to its logical conclusion. However, there are a number of caveats to be aware of. First, these suggestions relate to secondary pupils in Key Stage 3 and 4 and so would need to be adapted for use with younger pupils. Second, I have described the process in its absolute entirety; you may prefer to adopt a more informal approach that does not involve so many other formal contributions to the process. Third, but perhaps most important of all, is that simply because this system has worked for me, it will not necessarily be appropriate for you. Read through my suggested strategies; take from them what you will, and take full ownership of any system that you find works.

Stage 1: Identifying inappropriate behaviour

If you have read and inwardly digested the contents of this chapter it should be relatively easy to identify those pupils for whom the implementation of a behaviour plan would be appropriate. The types of youngsters you need to target are those for whom your classroom management plan has not worked, and where all your attempts to strike up good working relationships have failed. When I carried out a survey amongst newly qualified teachers and teacher trainees early in 2004 they came up with the following list of persistently annoying behaviours from some of their pupils:

- shouting out answers in class;
- making inappropriate and lewd comments;
- swearing;
- taunting or fighting with other pupils;
- constantly getting out of their seats and wandering around the classroom;
- being late for lessons and then making an entrance;
- talking to other pupils when the teacher is talking.

I am sure you will agree that these types of behaviour can have a negative effect on your relationships with the other pupils in the class and can finally erode your self-confidence and ability to teach well.

Stage 2: Setting up the process

As beginning teachers you need to be particularly careful about treading on other people's toes and you must, therefore, try to be sensitive to the work carried out by other members of your school team when you are preparing to put your plan into action. There are a number of people you need to consult before you set about implementing your behaviour plan. I have laid out in Figure 6.1 some of the questions that need to be addressed before you make arrangements to meet the pupil concerned.

Who do I need to consult with?	Discussion questions
Head of department	Does the behaviour of this pupil warrant a behaviour plan? Is your proposed strategy appropriate for this specific pupil? Have you used the assertive discipline policy consistently? Have you used the departmental sanctions to support your classroom discipline plan? Is this a battle you can win? Is the return likely to justify your investment?
Head of year	*All* of the questions shown above, plus:
Form tutor	Are there any relevant home background issues you should know about? Is there a pattern to the pupil's poor behaviour? Time of day/types of lesson, time of the week? Have you consulted your head of department? Have you kept head of year and form tutor informed of the issues?
SEN co-ordinator	Have you read the SEN files? Are you aware as to whether the pupil has got a medical condition and whether medication is being administered? If so, are you clear about the characteristics of this condition? Are you aware of the implications of this condition on the pupil's behaviour and learning?
Parents	Why have you contacted them? What can they do to aid the process? Do you want to know what the child is like at home? How can they reward successful outcomes?

Figure 6.1   Behaviour plan checklist

Stage 3: Meeting with the pupil

Before putting the behaviour management plan into operation, it is important to hold a formal meeting between you and the youngster for whom it is intended.

Building a rapport

If your behaviour plan is going to stand any chance of working, it is vital that you use the meeting to build up a rapport between the two of you. You will only be able to do this if the pupil feels comfortable in your presence. Find a quiet private space and give yourself plenty of time for the process. Try to make the youngster feel special. Provide them with a drink (and, if you are feeling generous, a few biscuits). Pay particular attention to establishing and maintaining a relaxed body posture and use a friendly and supportive tone of voice. Make sure that you outline the issues and session objectives to the pupil. Make sure that you stress that the session is all about looking for a way forward and that it is not simply about you taking an opportunity to criticise their behaviour. Ensure that the pupil knows that you are not there to make the issue personal! It is also very important to listen carefully to what the youngster is saying. Make sure that the youngster actually *sees* that you are listening. You can do this by repeating what they are saying and by re-framing their responses. You could say something like 'If I hear you correctly, what you are saying is ...' or, 'Let's see if I've got this right. The way you see the situation is ...' or, 'It is important to know how you feel in this situation. Judging by what you are telling me, you feel ...'.

Information gathering

One of the main reasons for the meeting is to find out exactly what is causing this pupil to behave in this inappropriate manner. Wherever possible, therefore, make your questions *open-ended* so that you can afford the pupil an opportunity to explore the reasons for behaving in this particular manner. Asking *closed* questions will restrict the pupils to talking about those issues that *you* have mapped out to be the cause of their disruptive behaviour. Remember that it is just as important to explore the emotions of the pupils as it is to establish the facts of the case. We discussed earlier in the chapter how pupils bring their own socially constructed agenda into the classroom with them. If you are having problems with particular pupils, it could simply be because their perspective about the way they are being treated is different from yours. Therefore, it is very important to take time to elicit the beliefs and perceptions of the pupils. Youngsters, to be able to modify their behaviour, have to know exactly what it is they are doing that *needs* changing, why they are behaving in this manner and how things look to other people. This process is called 'mirroring'. The initial part of the discussion should focus, therefore, on the reasons behind the pupil's anti-social behaviour. As we have already explored, very often the situation revolves around the issues of self-esteem and power. Your choice of language at this stage of the proceedings is vital. You will get absolutely nowhere if you simply start to read off a list of the pupil's faults. You need to involve the pupil as much as possible in the process, and get them to explore their own behaviour and the reasons behind their actions. As soon as you tell the pupil that you *know* the reasons for their misbehaviour, you have lost! Make sure, therefore, at this point that you *ask* or *suggest* but not *tell*. Using sentences such as:

> 'To me, bursting into the room once the lesson has started, shows that you might be seeking my attention? What do think about this?'

> 'You seem to be the type of person who needs to have some control over what you do. (That is not necessarily a bad thing.) Do you think that this could be one of the reasons why you don't like being told what to do?'

> 'I've got a suggestion to make about why you might be getting yourself into a bit of bother – let me share this with you and you can tell me what you think.'

Very often, the youngster is not fully aware of what their actions look like to other people and you should try to use this opportunity to demonstrate, or mirror their behaviour. First, it is very important that you ask the permission of the pupil to do this and, second, that you do not ridicule the youngster in any way.

Tempting as it is, you need to hold fire on giving any advice at this stage. You need to explain that the process involves the two of you working together towards gaining an agreed set of actions that will help to alleviate some of the anti-social behaviours exhibited by this pupil. However, it is imperative that the youngster comes to his or her own conclusions about the possible ways forward.

Setting goals and agreeing strategies

One of the main purposes of your dialogue with the pupil is to bring about a change in their behaviour. In order to do this, targets need to be set and goals need to be realised. It is very important to make these goals achievable but, if you feel that this is not going to be possible to do all in one go, you need to break each goal down into manageable, achievable and realistic sub-goals. For example, if you know that your pupil would find it difficult not to call out in class for an entire lesson, then break up the lesson into, say, ten-minute time slots and ask the pupil to keep a record of the number of complete time blocks he or she manages to control themselves. Let's take another example. A pupil in one of your classes cannot seem to stop swearing. You know no amount of nagging is really going to alter this behaviour. What do you do? Although I feel that extrinsic rewards are important, and I will mention these later, the youngster has got to be made aware of the benefits of behaving well. The first thing that needs to happen is that he or she must be informed of the damage this type of anti-social behaviour can do to his or her relationships and career prospects. As I mentioned earlier, the pupil also needs to be set manageable targets that will help to control any outbursts. Something that has worked for me is getting the pupil to use a self-regulatory pro-forma, marking as notches on a five bar gate, the number of times he or she has been just about to swear, but thought better of it. I know that the expression 'being taken for a ride' might be popping into many of your heads as you read this paragraph. Yes, this system does require you to trust in the individuals' wishes to change their behaviour. Yes, they could abuse the system very easily. However, isn't this just the point of the exercise? It is important to put some of the onus onto pupils to get them to think about the issue and to take some responsibility for their own behaviour. I would be lying if I said that I have had 100 per cent success with this method. When you take risks with youngsters like these, there are bound to be failures. However, I usually find that the most difficult ones are unhappy about the way they behave in lessons and are keen to do something about it. So, again, I keep trying. I use these self-regulatory sheets to deal with a number of annoying habits such as pupils swinging on their chairs; getting out of their seats; talking across the classroom to their friends.

Accessing resources

Although, when confronted, many difficult pupils recognise their own anti-social behaviour, very few of them have the confidence to tackle their problems on their own, or feel they have the resources to bring about a modification of their behaviours. Your role within these initial sessions is to convince the youngster that he or she does have the skills and qualities to turn things around. This is where really knowing your pupils comes into play. My research into the under-achievement of boys revealed that, in out-of-school contexts, many of these youngsters do display many of the skills and qualities we are desperately trying to encourage in school. Take Marc, Robert, Alistair and Colin for example. A bigger bunch of rogues you simply couldn't ask for. These pupils were simply the bane of many a teacher's life. They were constantly absent or late, rarely handed work in on time, were often rude and aggressive and were generally extremely unco-operative. In talking to them, however, I discovered that Marc was a ballroom dancing champion, Stuart got up at 5.45 a.m. to do a paper round, Alistair worked all day Saturdays in his dad's motor repair shop and Colin was captain of the school football team. Figure 6.2 shows an amalgamation of the skills and qualities of these four lads. I am sure you will agree that this list is quite impressive.

Qualities	Skills
Reliability	Motor co-ordination skills
Conscientiousness	Musical skills
Perseverance and staying power	Problem-solving skills
Ability to work with others	Leadership skills
Approachability	Communication skills
Loyalty	Physical skills

Figure 6.2:   Qualities and skills audit

My advice would, therefore, be to use your meeting time to audit pupils' successes, both in and out of school, to use these examples to build up their self-esteem and to get the message across that they do have it in them to take control over their lives in school. As we know, a lack of self-esteem is very often the issue and this type of pupil will struggle to come up with things they are successful at. You may, therefore, have to be highly proactive in initiating the process. Things you could focus on might be:

- a successful work experience placement;
- their membership of a school or local sports team;
- any community work they might do;
- part-time jobs;
- hobbies and interests;
- outside school club;
- drama, music, dance productions in school or the community;
- their roles within the family, e.g. do they act as carers?.

Rehearsing success

This is quite a difficult thing for many youngsters to do. The process requires them to create a visual image of how they are going to change their behaviour in school, and what life could be like if they were able to achieve this. It also requires them to rehearse internally their responses to specific classroom scenarios, and to start thinking about how they can also transfer these newly-found skills to other challenging situations. Through the process of role-play you can coach the youngster into acting appropriately in lessons. Let me give you a brief example of where this strategy has been implemented in my school. A number of teachers voiced their concern to the special educational needs co-ordinator about the way a small group of youngsters behaved when they entered and left their classrooms. These pupils would arrive just a few minutes late each time – not late enough for the teacher to create a major fuss about it, but late enough to disturb the teacher's flow and to break the concentration of the other pupils in the class. They would come into the room and fling their bags down on the table and say something like: 'Hi, Miss, how are you? Sorry we're late, Miss, we had to get a drink. What we doing today?' They would leave the room in a similarly robust manner. Although I am sure you will agree there is nothing particularly malicious about this behaviour, you will appreciate that the regularity of this occurrence was both annoying and stressful to the teachers concerned. It had got to the stage where these teachers were beginning to build up an increasing level of resentment towards this group of pupils. The special educational needs co-ordinator had first to get these youngsters to understand how their behaviour made the teachers and the rest of the pupils in the class actually feel. He did this by mirroring their actions and showing them how this behaviour appeared to the other pupils in the class. He then asked these youngsters to talk about an activity or hobby that was important to them or to describe one of their favourite television programmes. Once the children had finished doing this, he then asked them to imagine what they would feel like if their brothers or sisters constantly interrupted their activities or their programme. Having done all this, he booked the drama room and got the youngsters to carry out a number of role play exercises that involved them in practising making an orderly entrance and exit to and from a classroom. Although it is fair to say that these youngsters continued to be difficult in lessons, the subject teachers reported a dramatic improvement in this specific aspect of their behaviour. I am not suggesting for one minute that you go to such lengths in your attempts to get your difficult youngsters to rehearse their newly modified responses but I hope this example gives you an idea of the sort of thing you can do to help pupils change their behaviour. However, when everything else has failed, that may be the time to try a more creative approach to solving the problem.

What does a behaviour management plan look like?

The answer to this question is quite simple; it is entirely up to you what your plan looks like. There are however some guiding principles you may wish to employ when designing the final document. You need to devise a plan that identifies the pupil's targets clearly and that it is written in language they are able to understand. The plan must also be easy to implement and must not run for too great a time. My experience shows me that the plan will lose impact after about three weeks. The other thing you might like to do in order to give the process a degree of formality and status, is to include a pupil/teacher contract. I have provided an example for you in Figure 6.3, but please do not see this as being set in stone. You need to adapt your plan according to the situation and the needs of the individual pupil.

Although earlier we explored the intrinsic benefits to the pupils of behaving appropriately in lessons, this on its own is often not enough to motivate pupils to modify a behaviour pattern that has sometimes taken years to become established. It is imperative that you initiate a reward system. I, therefore, strongly advise you to

- use plenty of verbal praise;
- use the school's reward system;
- inform other relevant members of staff, for example, head of year, form tutor etc;
- telephone or write to parents informing them of their child's progress;
- issue privileges to the pupil, for example, half an hour on the computer;
- use departmental funds to purchase some confectionary or a gift voucher.

What happens if you feel you have tried everything? You have got to know your pupils well, you have made particular efforts to strike up and maintain good relationships with your challenging youngsters and you have set up individual behaviour management plans with some, or all, of them. However, despite doing all this, the behaviour of one or two individual pupils in your classes is still challenging and unacceptable. Where do you go from here?

Perhaps one of the hardest things to accept for any conscientious teacher, but particularly for those more idealistic teachers in the dawn of their careers, is that you can't win them all. That is not to say you should adopt a defeatist attitude and stop trying. However, you do need to be realistic about what you are able, and are not able, to achieve in your first few years of teaching. This could, therefore, now be the time for you to pass the issue on to your head of department and for him or her to lend some weight to the proceedings. Heads of department and heads of year, however, can get extremely frustrated when members of staff abdicate responsibility for their pupils and refer them without making any real effort to implement the school's behaviour policy. If, though, you can convince them that you really

Behaviour management plan for pupil X

I have discussed my behaviour with the following members of staff:

Subject teacher	☑	(Pupil needs to tick the appropriate box)
Head of department	☑	
Head of year	☑	
Form tutor	☑	
Parents	☐	

and agree that there are certain aspects of my behaviour that are not acceptable. I agree to work with them in changing my behaviour.

These are things I need to work on
(To increase the pupil's ownership of the process they need to write this down in their own words. I have provided some examples of inappropriate behaviours for you. However be careful not to overload the pupil with targets.)

- Shouting out in class
- Swinging on chair
- Being out of my seat in lessons
- Being rude
- Losing my temper

How will I set about doing this?
(Again, this needs to be in 'pupil-speak' but I have given a few examples below.)

- I'll use my self-monitoring form to see how many times I stop myself shouting out/ swinging on my chair.
- I'll try to bring my own pen, pencil and ruler so I don't have to get out of my seat during lessons. If I need equipment I'll ask my teacher to bring it to me.
- When I feel that I am starting to lose my temper I will take a deep breath and count slowly from ten down to one. If there is a sink in the room I will ask if I can wash my face with cold water.

How will my teachers help me?
(It is necessary to brainstorm with staff the way the pupil could be supported. Again, I have put down a few suggestions below.)

- My teacher could give me some time-out when I am getting angry.
- My teacher could praise and encourage me when I am trying to improve.
- My teachers could talk to each other about how well I am doing.

Figure 6.3:   Behaviour management plan for pupil X (continued)

Comment Box

(Take every opportunity to praise the pupil for any progress made. However, if things haven't gone too well, try to make your comments as positive as possible by writing something like – 'Gary struggled to meet his targets today but I am looking forward to Monday's lesson where he can give it a fresh go'.)

Signed............................Pupil
Signed............................Subject teacher
Signed............................Head of department *
Signed............................Head of year *
Signed............................Form tutor *
Signed............................Parent *

> * You have to decide how formal to make your plan and whom to involve.

Figure 6.3:   Behaviour management plan for pupil X

have tried absolutely everything, but that you have reached the end of the road, then I feel confident that you will receive the support and encouragement you deserve. Before you take the big step and refer these pupils I suggest you document everything you have done up to the point of referral. The checklist in Figure 6.4 should be helpful.

You might find a number of actions are proposed: the youngster may be removed from the class permanently or may be taken out of your lessons for a temporary period of time. Tempting as it might be simply to get rid of the problem I would suggest that you initially opt for the latter strategy. Providing that opportunities are given to both parties to reflect on the issues in hand, this time-out period can often prove to be beneficial in helping to build bridges and re-establish your expectations. One thing I am absolutely certain of is your need to re-tain an element of control over proceedings. The youngster should *not* be allowed back into your class until there is an agreement to meet your basic expectations. I would suggest that prior to the pupil being re-admitted to your lessons, you arrange a meeting with the head of year or head of department, the pupil and yourself and that you prepare some clear written guidelines for this re-admittance. In order to exemplify exactly what I mean by this, I have included a transcript of a conversation I had with a Year 10 girl whom I had to temporarily exclude from my lessons for some outrageous anti-social behaviour. Again, this is not supposed to be a prescriptive list, but it has been

Strategies employed	Have done
Set up and implemented a classroom and behaviour management plan that consists of me formally setting out my own rules/routines/ expectations and gradated sanctions.	☑
Made maximum use of the school's assertive policy to support my discipline.	☑
Made every effort to strike up good relationships out of the classroom with my more challenging pupils.	☑
Formally interviewed these challenging pupils with a view to modifying their behaviour.	☑
Set up, implemented and evaluated a behaviour management plan with these youngsters.	☑

Figure 6.4: Strategy checklist

included simply as a means of illustrating the importance of maintaining an element of control in a difficult situation. It is important for a teacher to have the feeling of empowerment restored to them, especially in situations where they have felt particularly impotent.

'Hannah, I would like to welcome you back to the class. I am looking forward to working with you again. You need to know, however, that if you are to make a really fresh start you need to read through and accept my behaviour expectations. It is very important for you to understand that these expectations apply not *only* to you but to *every* other pupil in the class. It is important for you to:

- arrive promptly and adopt a low profile in the classroom;
- get your working equipment/books out and wait quietly until I am ready to start the lesson;
- not call out in class and/or make stupid comments;
- sit on your own when I am giving instructions or explaining the work. If things go well, I'll let you sit with a pupil of my choice;
- wait behind after the lesson to discuss anything that you are unhappy about;
- leave the room *without* arguing if I ask you to do so.'

You will notice from my choice of language in outlining the conditions for re-admittance that I have been extremely specific in my expectations. You should be able interpolate from these the nature of Hannah's anti-social behaviour.

In this chapter I have attempted to do a number of things. In the early part, I described what usually constitutes disruptive behaviour. I then went on to explore a number of different rationale as to why some pupils might choose to behave in such a challenging manner. Towards the end of this chapter, I have outlined a number of preventative measures you can take to help reduce the likelihood of disruptive behaviour in your lessons, before then going on to describe some supportive discipline techniques you could use when all else fails. I hope I have met the objective of the chapter which is to provide you as beginning teachers with somewhere else to go when all your discipline strategies have failed. I leave you in the final throes of this chapter with the following message. It can take a teacher many years to reach a stage in their career where pupil disruption is not a major concern. Even the most experienced and skilled of teachers are subject to anti-social behaviour which has a root cause well beyond their control. The message is clear; have high but realistic expectations and never stop trying!

Chapter 7

Running a Successful Tutor Group

'Morning, folks. Right, settle down, trainers and coats off, shoes on, turn your chairs this way, face me – come on, let us sort ourselves out, it's registration time. Absolute silence, please.' Pause, scan the classroom. 'That's excellent, thank you. I have a number of things to go through before we start the PHSE lesson, so, listen quietly and carefully. By the end of the lesson I need your log books up here please. Gemma, Richard – I need your absence notes for Monday. Craig, your mum phoned, you're to meet her in the main playground at 3.10 today – she forgot to tell you that you're booked in to see the dentist at 3.30. Martha, Mr Williams wants to see you now about the incident in Science yesterday. Hang on a minute, I'll have to write you out a pass. Andrew, can you give these letters out to the rest of the class. Oh, yes, I nearly forgot. There are nine of you who still owe me reply slips for your reports. Please bring them up here now otherwise you'll be staying in after school tomorrow. Laura, Sam – please don't forget that you are staying in after school this evening. Your PSHE wasn't done – remember? That reminds me, Mrs Murphy wants me to tell you your work-experience letters need to be in by the 28th. If you haven't done them, you must do these pretty quickly. If you want help then I will be in here at the end of the day. By the way, Darren, well done for your efforts in English. Let's have a look at what you have done. Aaron and Shaun, I need to see you outside for a couple minutes before we start the lesson. The rest of you are on trust while I am out of the room talking to these boys. Meanwhile, Emily, can you and Becky please give out the PSHE booklets and the exercise books so that we can make a start when I come back.' And so the tutor period begins.

As beginning teachers, many of you will already have taken on some responsibility for a tutor group, either by supporting the class tutor, or by taking sole charge of your own form. Inexperienced as you are, I am sure you have already begun to realise what a demanding role this is, and how important the form tutor is to the lives of their pupils. The purpose of this chapter is to explore the role of the form tutor which I believe to be one of the most difficult and complex jobs in the school. I have no doubt that a good form tutor has to be multi-skilled, flexible, physically and mentally robust, and comfortable in adopting an authoritative and democratic teaching style such as that described in Chapter 3.

As an experienced teacher, I still find it difficult to quantify everything I do as a form tutor. All I know is that, having carried out a mountain of tasks in such a short space of time, I very often come out of registration sessions and PSHE lessons absolutely shell-shocked.

The process of writing this book has afforded me the opportunity to step back and to think about the role of the form tutor in more detail. In doing this, I have come up with a number of broad job-description categories which I have placed in order of importance. However, the status of each category can vary according to the perspective of the school's headteacher. My headteacher, for example, sees the priority of the pastoral system within the school as being there mainly to support the academic development of the pupils. I, on the other hand, see the pastoral system as being there in its own right and, as you can see below, have put this at the top of my list. The form tutor's role therefore is to

- provide formal and informal opportunities for the personal and social development of pupils;
- provide an infrastructure to support the school's ethos on behaviour and attitudes;
- support pupils' academic progress;
- act as a conduit for those communications between school and home.

Figure 7.1 overleaf shows the full extent of your role as a form tutor. Looks onerous, doesn't it? Don't panic! It is my intention to work through the five categories shown in the figure and to offer guidance and advice on a number of issues associated with these specific form tutoring roles.

Providing formal and informal opportunities for the personal and social development of your pupils

I wonder how many of you have actually thought about the ultimate aim of a good form tutor. Allow me to share my own view of this with you. I feel that the overriding aim of the form tutor should be to create well-balanced, socially and morally competent pupils, who are able to realise their full learning potential and lead happy lives. Figure 7.1 shows how this can be done. Although this may sound rather idealistic, my premise is that if you begin your career with this view in mind, you will at least start off on the right track. Believe you me, you will not get all of it right all of the time, but at least you will be clear about the route which you wish to take with your pupils.

At the beginning of each year with my form group, I make sure that I reinforce my rules, routines and expectations. I also refer them to the illustrations shown on page 129 and 130 to explain my form tutoring role to the pupils. My explanation is based upon the work on personality by the psychologist Sigmund Freud.

Supporting academic progress
Checking homework diaries
Rewarding academic achievement
Checking and reporting on academic progress
Contacting parents on academic matters
Target-setting
Supporting subject tutors
Contacting parents about academic matters.

Supporting the personal and social development of the pupils
Teaching personal and health education
Organising form trips and events
Chairing form meetings
Collecting monies for charity events.

Supporting child on an individual basis
Counselling pupils experiencing difficulties
Helping to move pupils on
Referring pupils to other people/organisations

Supporting the school's stance on attitudes and behaviour
Acting as a mouthpiece for the school's behaviour and attitude policy. Clarifying and
  implementing school rules
Supporting school's policy on punctuality, attendance and uniform
Rewarding good behaviour through credit system
Imposing sanctions on pupils who contravene school rules, e.g. giving detentions,
  contacting parents.

Aiding communication between school and home
Distributing letters to go home to parents
Collecting reply slips
Passing on information to pupils.

Figure 7.1: The role of the form tutor

I explain to my pupils that my role is to be responsible for taking them from the id stage of their personality through to the superego stage. I tell them that the id stage relates to the side of their personality that has a tendency simply to take what it wants. This stage is typical of most young children, but can also be seen in many older

youngsters who at this stage of their lives do not have a completely developed conscience.

Moving on, I then go on to explain that the ego stage represents the part of us that motivates us to commit an immoral act if we think we are unlikely to get caught. This is the stage where most youngsters in your tutor group will be, that is, they know the broad difference between right and wrong but, given the opportunity, will go ahead and make some questionable moral decisions at times.

Finally, the ultimate goal, that of the superego stage, represents the truly moral being where a person has obtained a fully developed conscience and where true altruism reigns.

Of course, it is not as simple as this. I explain to the pupils that humans are complex beings and that these stages in our personal, social and moral development are by no means clearly defined. It is important for pupils to realise that, even as adults, the id sometimes tends to prevail and we start to behave selfishly when we do not get our own way. I then go on to explain to them that sometimes it is the ego which tends to dominate our behaviour, and that we often do things we know to be wrong, only ceasing this behaviour when we know we are likely to get caught. As form tutors, you need to think about this before you start to take the moral high ground with your pupils when admonishing them for their misdemeanours. How often, for instance, when you have been speeding, have you slowed down when you have spotted a police car? How often have you taken the odd roll of sticky tape from work? How often have you told a lie to get yourself out of a tricky situation? The list can be endless.

Of course, the superego comes into play with some people more than others, Most of us, at times, are capable of carrying out altruistic acts, where the only reward gained is simply knowing that we have done the right thing. Although I am no psychologist, I have found that this simple model has helped to outline my aims to my tutor group. I have also used this several times with some particularly challenging and self-centred pupils in the past. It has helped these youngsters to understand their behaviour and to rectify some of their more selfish traits for the benefit of the other pupils in the class. Try it, and see what you think!

In Chapter 5, we briefly explored the functions of the reptilian brain and described how our knowledge of this part of the brain can relate to our classroom practice. I am in no doubt, whatsoever, that understanding how the reptilian brain and the limbic system works can most certainly help you to become a better form tutor. As we know, the reptilian brain is the primeval part of the brain responsible for routine body functions which operate continually outside our conscious awareness, such as breathing, heart beat, blood pressure, temperature, balance, and so on. It is also responsible for our survival responses, as for example the fight or flight response in the face of danger. This is the part of the brain that seeks physical and emotional security. Pupils need *somewhere* and *someone* to run to when things go badly for them. Creating a form room that is bright, comfortable and secure from *outside* threats is an important role for the form tutor. Simply controlling who comes into your form room at break and lunchtimes, and making yourself available to these youngsters when they need you, can really enhance your relationships with them.

Shaw and Hawes (1998) wrote about how we all have a pre-disposition towards social conformity – including hierarchies and pecking order. Despite thousands of years of evolution we still conform to rote and ritual. Hopefully you will now begin to understand fully the need to establish rules and routines during your registration and PSHE sessions. In this way you will be providing these youngsters with the security needed for *real* learning to take place.

The limbic system is the part of the brain that concerns itself with governing our emotions, and lies at the very heart of our beliefs, values and sense of identity. It is also important to note that this part of the brain contains our long-term memory. As we have seen in Chapter 2, the more a teacher engages the emotions of a pupil, the more likely the material is likely to be embedded in the long-term memory of the child, and the quicker and easier it can be recalled. Obviously, having this knowledge is imperative for subject teachers, but it is also very important for teachers carrying out a pastoral role.

So, how, in practical terms, can we utilise our knowledge of the brain to develop our relationships with our pupils? The first thing to suggest is that you endeavour to create a corporate sense of identity within your tutor group. Build up the notion that this is the best form in the year group and try to create a sense of pride in being a member of this class. You can do this in a number of ways. Take every opportunity to take your pupils out on form trips. It does not have to be far, nor does it have to be over-ambitious. You could take them to the local swimming pool and for a burger at a nearby fast food restaurant. If you live in a town with a professional football team you could get cheap booking rates and take them to see a match. You could take them ice/roller skating, paint-balling or to a local theme park or to see a show. Quite honestly, it does not really matter what you do, because the youngsters will simply enjoy being out with each other and with you! I have found that taking pupils out on form trips, especially in Year 7, has proved to be a major investment in helping me to build up good relationships with my tutor group. There have been times, later on in their school careers, when I have had to deal firmly with some of these youngsters and I am convinced that it was all the hard work carried out earlier on, that created an infrastructure of trust between us, and that allowed these pupils to accept this discipline with good grace. I also never cease to be amazed at what I learn about my youngsters during the informal chats I have with them on these trips. I discovered on one particular trip, for example, that Andrew, Ben and Peter all played the guitar, that Helen trained with the England net-ball team and that Samantha took part in amateur theatrical pro-ductions. As a result I find myself continually renegotiating my image of these youngsters.

Building up happy memories for pupils is a vital part of form tutoring. One of the things I did with a tutor group was to produce a scrapbook of memories for each of the five years they were with me. These books were comprised of photographs I had taken of my pupils at school and on trips, and local newspaper cuttings that related to my youngsters. It was very rewarding to see many of my pupils flicking through the pages of these books during break or registration and re-calling the fun times they had in earlier years. They certainly provided a topic of conversation and have done a lot to create that all important

team spirit and sense of *oneness* within the tutor group. At the end of five years, I did two things: first, carried out a free raffle draw so that five pupils could each take one year book home with them; second, invited parents and pupils in to attend a special commemorative evening for my form. (I scanned most of the photographs, to be presented on PowerPoint as part of the evening of celebration and farewell to my tutor group.) Something you could also do is to find out when your youngsters are taking part in school sports, or musical or drama productions. Just turning up to watch these pupils means a tremendous amount to them and helps to create that all-important bond required for a successful tutor group. Whether *you* do something like this with *your* tutor group is not the issue. The whole point of describing to you what I do is to get you to think about what you could do to create a sense of identity within your own tutor group.

In Chapter 5, and in my previous book (Dixie, 2003), I discussed at length the effect of the physical layout of the classroom on the mood and behaviour of the pupils. A great deal of research has been carried out to show how the layout and condition of the classroom can have a marked effect on the work ethic, behaviour and attitudes of pupils. This effect should not be underestimated! If you take care of your surroundings, and if you encourage your pupils to do the same, then you will go a long way to creating a positive ethos and sense of pride in your classroom.

Suggestion

Encourage the pupils to bring their own posters in for display. Display work they have done in other subjects, for example, artwork, poetry, ICT assignments. Use bright paper to cover display boards. Wallpaper borders make effective surrounds. Plants often lend a calming effect. Make sure that you establish a form notice board. You also need to appoint form monitors. Establish a *form* identity.

Obviously, one of the main aims of any form tutor is to get to know your pupils. Take time to talk to each and every one of them individually to find out what motivates them. Keep records of your conversations and of the things they do out of school. Talk to the youngsters about their hobbies and interests, take the time to show an interest in them as people. You could use a questionnaire to act as a focus for discussion. Try not to restrict your conversations to the most approachable members of your form. Make an effort to involve all pupils in your group activities. Keep your eyes open and pay attention to detail. Most pupils really do like it when you comment on their contributions to school life. It illustrates that you have noticed them and their achievements. You do, however, need to be very aware of the issue of disclosure and it is absolutely vital that you warn your pupils that you may have to pass on sensitive information to their head of year or to another appropriate adult.

Suggestion

You could build up a series of profiles of the pupils in your form. Pupils could produce their own personal fact sheets that could be displayed in your classroom.

Suggestion

A brief complimentary comment on a youngster's performance in a school play, on the football pitch or for a good piece of work they have done, goes a long way to making them feel good. Be careful where and how you praise the pupil as you could embarrass him or her if your comments are too public.

I have expounded in some detail the need for creating a sense of well-being and security in your tutor group. All of this is fine, but remember that your job as a teacher is to find ways to extend these youngsters. As a form tutor you need to find opportunities constantly to challenge your pupils emotionally and socially. To do this, you must get to know your pupils very well. Knowing when to challenge them and when simply to let things be is an integral part of form tutoring. The quotation below summarises the skill needed to maintain a balanced approach towards your youngsters.

Taking a class is like playing a salmon – a slight change of direction here, a discreet tightening of the line there, and so on. If you are too insensitive, you will not only break the line but lose the fish as well. (Source unknown)

In order to establish real class unity, it is very important to avoid pupils being polarised into cliques. Make sure that, on occasions, you mix your pupils up during PSHE lessons. They may not be entirely happy to start with, but if you do this early enough in Year 7 they will accept this procedure as the norm.

Suggestion

On occasions you should try to create mixed ability and mixed gender groupings. You could also group your pupils according to their preferred learning styles. Perhaps you could produce some ready-made name cards that can easily be put in each place before the pupils arrive at your lesson. Another light-hearted way of grouping your pupils is to distribute playing cards randomly. Pupils holding the same cards sit and work together for that lesson.

Suggestion

You might like to put aside some time a week when members of your form can simply come and chat with you. You might like to tell them when your duty day is so that they can walk with you and have a chat.

Knowing when to step in is a very important skill and only you can determine when, and whether, to intervene in social issues that arise between your pupils. One of the main threats to a harmonious tutor group is the damage that can be caused by rumour and gossip. I feel so strongly about this that I have displayed a poster in my classroom with the following slogan.

The most dangerous thing in the world is *gossip*!

As form tutors you do have a duty to reduce conflict within your classroom, and to help the pupils to deal with gossip and rumour-mongering. My advice would be to try to get the youngsters to sort things out for themselves first, but if this fails, you need to take on a mediating or troubleshooting role. However, you must remember to remain objective and to be very careful not to get embroiled in the issue. I was flicking through a coverless magazine when I came across a story that I thought would be very useful in helping my youngsters deal with hurtful gossip, rumour and hearsay. As you will see, the story refers to something called the 'triple filter test'.

A Socratic lesson

In ancient Greece, Socrates was famous for holding the pursuit of knowledge in the highest esteem. One day a man bumped into him and said: 'Socrates, let me tell you what I heard about your friend.'
'First,' Socrates replied, 'I'd like you to pass the triple filter test. Take a moment to filter what you are about to say. The first filter is truth. Are you sure what you heard is true?'

'No,' the man said. 'Actually I just heard about it and ...'

'So, you don't know whether it is true or not,' Socrates replied. 'Now let's try the filter of goodness. Is what you're about to say about my friend something good?'

'No, on the contrary ...'

'So,' Socrates continued, 'you want to tell me something bad, but you're not certain it's true. You may still pass the test though. Lastly, there's the filter of usefulness. Is what you are going to tell me going to be useful to me?'

'No, not really.'

'Well,' concluded Socrates, 'if what you want to say isn't true, good or useful, then why would you want to tell me at all?'

This is why Socrates was a great philosopher and held in such high esteem. It also explains why he never found out his friend was having an affair with his wife! (Source unknown)

Once the laughter has died down, I use this story to illustrate to the pupils how to deal with rumour, hearsay and gossip. Whenever I hear of my pupils spreading gossip or half-truths I refer them to a poster (illustrated below) on my wall and ask them to think long and hard about what they are saying and doing, and whether they would pass the triple filter test.

The Triple Filter Test

Is what you are saying:

True?
Good?
Useful?

Would you pass the triple filter test?

One of the hardest things I have had to do in my role as form tutor is to try to pick up the pieces after pupils have been feuding with each other over a long period of time. In situations such as these, it is very important to remain neutral and to let each party know that you believe both of them to be sincere about their perceptions of the issues that lie at the heart of the conflict. I say perceptions, because this is exactly what they are. Each child will have his or her own social construction of the truth and no matter how hard you try, you may ultimately have to accept that you will never be able to get one pupil to understand fully the perspective of the other.

In cases such as these, you need to be able to talk your youngsters through these issues and get them to rehearse ways of avoiding situations that might lead to further conflict. Allow me to share with you one such situation that occurred with a girl who was in my Year 9 tutor group. For the purposes of anonymity, I have called her Maria. She and another girl, let's call her Kim, had been experiencing serious problems with each other for nearly a year. It finally got to the point where the two of them ended up scrapping like alley cats in public. The issue was referred to their head of year, who ended up getting the two sets of parents together to discuss the matter. No matter what the head of year suggested to help these youngsters solve the problem, nothing was resolved, and the situation soon reached an *impasse*. It was obvious to me that, unless something was done pretty quickly, we would soon have another fight on our hands. All it was going to take was a look or a passing comment by one or both of the girls and we would have two school exclusions on our hands. I took Maria out of one of her lessons and spent half an hour rehearsing a number of strategies that would help her to cope when she met up with Kim again. I took the opportunity actually to model some acceptable and unacceptable responses. This was an important thing to do because, as we have already seen, body language, voice tone and degree of eye contact are all important elements in helping to reduce or to inflame conflict. The text below provides the basis of a letter I wrote to Maria's mother and head of year outlining to them what action I had taken on the matter.

I have spoken to Maria at length about the incident that happened after school yesterday and have suggested a number of strategies she could use to cope in conflict situations such as these. I realise that in expecting her to deal successfully with this type of situation, I am asking a lot of a 13-year-old. I have told Maria that if she manages to gain these skills by the time she is an adult, she will have done extremely well. I have to say that Maria was extremely positive about the whole process and is willing to give it a go.

- Keep your facial expression and body language as neutral as possible. Do not sneer, do not look down your nose at the other person.
- Give yourself and the other person time and space to consider the issue and to think about the other person's perspective. You could say something like: 'We are both angry, give me some time to think about what you are saying.' *Never* try to deal with issues when you are angry; it will only make things worse. Walk away!
- Get rid of the audience! They will only make things worse and you will find it difficult to back down in public.
- If things are bad and you need an adult to act as a negotiator then come and see me.
- Accept that there will always be personality conflicts. If you don't get on – accept it, be pleasant to each other, but don't keep going back for more!
- Accept that you will not get things right every time.
- Avoiding conflict takes a lot of skill and maturity – you will not acquire these skills overnight!

The very best of luck, Maria.

Maria and her mum were very pleased with the practical advice offered and I am happy to report that, apart from one or two hiccups, Maria has been very successful in avoiding conflict with Kim.

You will remember in Chapter 4 that I described the need for teachers to be continually reflective about their teaching. I would, again, urge you constantly to evaluate your role as form tutor. Do not be afraid to canvass the opinions of your pupils, but do so in the wider context of the whole group working together to explore ways to improve the smooth running of the form. Also, again, you should not become despondent if things do not always go smoothly. Similarly, as with subject teaching, if you get things right 80 per cent of the time I would deem this as real success.

Providing an infrastructure to support the school's behaviour and attitudes policy

In my role as professional development tutor, I often sit on interview panels whose responsibility it is to appoint newly qualified teachers to the school. One of my headteacher's favourite questions is to ask the candidates to define the role of the form tutor. Most candidates can come up with responses that generally relate to the form tutor's role in supporting their pupils both pastorally and academically, but very few are able to deliver the answer he is really looking for, that the form tutor should act as a conduit for the transference of the beliefs, values and attitudes of the school.

Every school should have a behaviour and attitudes policy. It is very important for you as beginning teachers to understand your role in helping to implement this. You can do this at the beginning of the year when you go through the school rules with your pupils. No one is asking you to agree with all the rules, but it is absolutely imperative that you do your utmost to present a cohesive and unified approach to the pupils by implementing these rules fairly and consistently.

All too often I hear struggling teachers bemoaning the fact that discipline in the school has really gone down the drain and that the management ought to do something about this. However, as far as I am concerned, they have missed the point. Each and every one of us has a responsibility to impart the values, norms and expectations of the school to the pupils we meet during the school day. It is important for us to remember that a strong school is a school where staff all work together to meet a common aim. As the saying goes, 'a chain will always break at its weakest link'. The message is simple – do not become that weakest link!

So, what exactly can you do to make a full contribution to the ethos of the school? I am suggesting that you start to consider your tutor periods and your PSHE lessons as microcosms of the school community and use these to promote a positive ethos amongst the pupils in your tutor group. If pupils leave your registration session not having been given the right messages for the day, and in the wrong frame of mind then, quite simply, the buck stops with you! You will appreciate, therefore, how important it is to get your registrations and PSHE lessons right as far as classroom and behaviour management issues are concerned.

I have written at length (Dixie, 2003) about the need to set up clear rules, routines and expectations with pupils. The registration session is the ideal opportunity for you to set up your pupils for the day. The first thing you need to do is to call for silence. I like to use a countdown system from three down to one because it gives the youngsters a brief moment to finish off what they are saying. Once, however, I am ready to take the register then the rule is simple; silence must prevail. I would be an absolute liar if I said that this system is foolproof. Youngsters do try it on, and do try to have a crafty word with their neighbours whilst I am taking the register. In order to cater for this, I have a slogan which I refer to at the beginning of every registration session; 'Quiet or clear up'. What this means is that if I catch a pupil talking during the registration process, they know that they are going to have to join me at the end of the day to help to clear up my classroom. Call it 'community service' if you like. Some of you reading this might possibly think that this approach might be a little over the top. However, if a teacher wants to establish and maintain good order in their classroom, there is a need for them to gain a *psychological edge* over the youngsters in their classes. In my opinion, here we have a situation which is absolutely shouting out for the implementation of firm rules and routines. To be strictly honest, any teacher will tell you that you do not actually need silence to take a register. You could simply scan the room and place a tick or a nought in the attendance box without the pupils even being aware that you are doing this. So why make a big deal about getting the youngsters quiet? I feel that obtaining silence is important for a number of reasons. In my registration sessions, I ask the pupils to take their coats off, put their school shoes on, sit down on a chair, face the front of the class and make eye contact with me whilst I am taking the register. Doing this conveys the message to the pupils that it is I, and not they, who determines what happens in my classroom. I also feel that by imposing some sense of order at the beginning of the day, I am doing my bit for my colleagues who will come across these pupils later on. Finally, because I am legally bound to produce accurate attendance records for the local educational authority, I need to make sure I do not make mistakes when I am taking the register. Mistakes can happen easily in a noisy classroom.

I have explained how implementing the advice given above can benefit the ethos of the school, but surely this book is all about getting on with kids! The question you may be asking, however, is how does this affect my relationships with pupils? The answer is simple. You read in Chapter 4 how perceptive and demanding the pupils were of their teachers. Most youngsters, despite often giving off signals to the contrary, know what is right and wrong. They demand and expect their teachers to impose a sense of order on their lives at a time when they sometimes struggle to understand facets of their own behaviour, and/or when they find it difficult to control themselves. In short, they want their teachers to act as their *conscience* until such a time when they can fully exercise their own.

A few important tips

- Registrations and PSHE lessons are all about power and control. They are symbols to show who is in charge.
- What you do now will have definite consequences for the future.
- Don't be lulled into a false sense of security. There will be a honeymoon period. Try to project yourself two or three years on when these youngsters will start to test you.

There will be occasions when pupils are reported to you for misbehaving in other lessons. You will have to find that fine balance between supporting your pupils and supporting the member of staff who has complained to you. Very often, in situations such as these, the truth lies somewhere between the two perspectives and you will have to steer a careful course, making sure that both parties feel they have been treated impartially. If it is obvious that your youngster has simply been out of order, then you need to follow up on their bad behaviour. I would suggest that in cases of repeated misbehaviour, you support your colleagues by issuing your own sanctions. It is, of course, equally important to reward instances of good or improved behaviour and you can do that through the school's formal reward process or by using your own system.

Adopt strategies for the future

- Establish firm routines during registrations. Provide verbal or visual symbols for the onset of the registration process.
- Insist on absolute silence whilst the register is being taken. Give pupils the rationale for doing this.
- Insist that all pupils are seated in their proper places during registration.
- Insist that they are suitably dressed in uniform, check footwear, insist they take coats off.
- Think carefully about your sanctions before you impose them – make them transparent, realistic and try to graduate them by degrees.
- Give pupils a degree of freedom but make sure they know who is in charge.

Providing academic support for your pupils

How can you as beginning teachers and form tutors support the academic progress of the pupils in your tutor group? The first thing I would advise is to gather evidence which will help you to provide an academic profile of your pupils. Using prior assessment data which usually contain such things as reading and mathematics scores, standard assessment tests results, and, in some cases, information about the learning styles of the individuals concerned, you need to build up a central set of records. You could store this material either on a database on your laptop or you could simply use a hardback folder. What is absolutely vital, however, is that you always have this data to hand when you need to make informed decisions about the youngsters in your class. It is, for example, always very useful to have this data when dealing with parents at consultation evenings.

Long before the first progress checks and/or reports are issued, you will begin to get an inkling of those pupils in your class who are under-achieving. Informal conversations in the staffroom with subject staff often reveal a lot about the way things are going for some of your pupils. Sometimes subject tutors will write to you formally informing you of their concern for individuals in your classes. Do not ignore these early warnings. My advice to you here would be to follow up on this by sending out a round robin circular to find out whether similar patterns of under-achievement or misbehaviour are occurring in other subject areas. It is important, however, to make sure that you study the prior assessment data before you interview the child. Having this data available will help you to make a judgement on whether these teachers have realistic expectations of this youngster. After weighing up the situation, you might find out that the youngster is simply un-able to cope with the work being set and this may be the message which you are going to have to convey to his subject teachers. Talking with, rather than to, the youngster will give you a clearer indication of the nature of the problem and will help you both to move the situ-ation on. However, it may turn out to be the case that the pupil is under-achieving *across the board* and that something needs to be done about this. Many form tutors, at this stage, might be tempted simply to inform their head of year and leave things at that. I need to stress very strongly that, at this stage, *you*, and not the head of year, are the best person to deal with this issue. Obviously you need to keep them fully informed, and to seek advice from them regularly, but *you* see the pupil daily and have a much more intimate knowledge of what makes him or her tick. Making an investment now will do absolute wonders for your relationship, not only with this pupil, but also with the other members of the class. I would then suggest that you offer to take on the mentoring of this individual for a specific period of time. Don't panic, this is not necessarily an onerous task, for it would only involve you meeting the youngster, say twice a term, reviewing the comments made by subject staff and then setting targets for the indivi-dual concerned. Very often youngsters, no matter how bright they are, do not know *how* to learn and you could use some of the interview time to discuss learning strategies with them. With the head of year's permission you should try to involve the child's parents in the process in order to make sure that everybody is singing from the same hymn sheet, co-operating with each other in their support for the youngster. Parents may also like to contribute to the process by helping their children to organise their time efficiently and by offering external rewards to the youngsters for making good progress. Whatever the outcome, I am absolutely sure that, by doing this, your relationship with that pupil and their parents will be dramatically improved.

I have described what you could do for individual pupils who, because of their poor achievement or behaviour record, have had their names brought to your notice. It is, of course, vital, however, that you carry out this academic monitoring process with *all* of the pupils in your class. You need to spend some time gaining an overview of pupil performance by reviewing their progress checks and subject reports. Try to make it your policy to interview each pupil as often as possible to find out how things are going. Endeavour to help the youngster by suggesting learning strategies and by setting them individual targets.

Homework is always a contentious issue with parents and pupils alike. You can certainly play your part in helping the pupils to adopt a positive and organised approach towards their work by checking their homework diaries regularly. What I tend to do is to give my young-sters a two-day window to bring their diaries in for me to sign. My rule is simple – if the diary is not signed by parents and presented to me within this two-day slot then the pupil will do a twenty minute detention at lunchtime. Those of you starting with more senior tutor groups might struggle to impose such a system, especially if their previous form tutor has not bothered too much about this, but it will be a lot easier for you to realise your expectations with the younger pupils. What is absolutely vital, however, is that you are consistent in your expectations and that you always carry out your sanctions with-out fail. I have to say that this is a lot easier said than done. At the be-ginning of this chapter, I described the first five minutes or so of a tutor period. When you are tired and absolutely rushed off your feet, you will find it tempting to opt out of this system but if you do give up on this process, you will not be able to recoup the situation at a later date. If you are consistent and fair in your approach with these younger pupils, then you will experience very little opposition to the system as the pupils move up into the senior school. The pupils will have become accustomed to your rules, routines and expectations. They will therefore see the process as simply being part and parcel of being a member of your form.

Acting as a conduit for communications between school and home

As form tutor, you are responsible for making sure that the pupils and their parents know what is going on. This means insisting that letters are taken home and that reply slips are returned for each and every pupil in your charge. As with my system of collecting in homework diaries or logbooks, I give my pupils a deadline to meet for returning their reply slips. Failure to meet these deadlines simply means that these youngsters have to do community service at the end of the day. As a result, I have got the tidiest classroom in the school!

So, having read this chapter, the two big questions you need to ask yourself is what sort of form tutor are you now and what sort do you want to be? Figure 8.1 is a checklist to help you to decide. Work through it and then ask yourself how you fared.

	Yes	No
Do you arrive on time for registration?	☐	☐
Do you arrive well-prepared?	☐	☐
Do you respect your pupils?	☐	☐
Do you expect to receive respect from your pupils?	☐	☐
Do you treat your pupils as individuals?	☐	☐
Do you smile and greet the pupils?	☐	☐
Do you utilise the pupils' problems as opportunities to move them on socially, emotionally, academically?	☐	☐
Are you a good listener?	☐	☐
Do you set high standards?	☐	☐
Do you apply rules and routines consistently?	☐	☐
Do you use punishment sparingly?	☐	☐
Do you avoid blanket punishments?	☐	☐
Do you deal with the misbehaviour of your pupils in other classes?	☐	☐
Do you extend and motivate your pupils?	☐	☐
Do you enjoy the company of your tutor group?	☐	☐
Do you really know your pupils well?	☐	☐
Do you display your pupils' work?	☐	☐
Do you look for ways to avoid confrontation?	☐	☐
Do you avoid humiliating pupils?	☐	☐
Do you avoid sarcasm?	☐	☐

Figure 8.1: What sort of form tutor are you?

Chapter 8

Conclusion

I have written this book because of my strong interest in all issues relating to classroom life. In Dixie (2003), I focused mainly on the *technical* aspects of behaviour management, offering readers a whole range of tactical strategies designed to get their pupils to behave in lessons. Important as these strategies are, they are not enough on their own to produce motivated, well-rounded, happy pupils, who are keen to learn, and willing to be reflective about themselves as social and moral beings. This book has taken things a stage further, by looking at the way good and bad teachers interact with pupils. It explores the consequences of these interactions and offers the reader a range of strategies designed to help improve teacher/pupil relationships.

I believe that this book should be of real practical value, not only to beginning teachers, but to all those who have taken the time to read it. In Chapter 1, I explained to you that my remit was to write about *real* teachers, *real* kids and *real* learning scenarios. As far as possible, this book has been evidence-based, drawing on my primary and secondary research data, and on my own experiences in the classroom. It was my intention to keep the theoretical side to a minimum and to provide you with practical advice and guidance about how to cope with a range of typical classroom scenarios. I hope you feel that I have realised this intention.

As you will no doubt have noted, there is a strong theme of reflective practice running throughout this book. It is important to stress, yet again, that the ideas and strategies offered are not to be seen as prescriptive. These methods have worked well for me over the years but it is up to you to adapt and temper these to suit your own personality, teaching style and the needs of your pupils. Although I am confident that I have furnished you with a number of potentially workable strategies that will help to improve your relationships with pupils, I hope that I have succeeded in getting you to ask the right questions. The fundamental tenet behind these questions should be that of establishing mutual respect and rapport with the pupils in your classes so that real learning can take place.

How exactly can you evaluate and quantify the quality of your relationships with your pupils? This is certainly a difficult task. I wrote in Chapter 4 about the need for you to canvass the opinions of youngsters about your teaching. By doing this, you will be able to gain some idea of their reactions to you and your teaching style. It is, however, fair to say that much of the time your assessment will be intuitive. It will not be long before you get a pretty good idea of what your pupils think of you. You will know this by observing their every-day responses and by the way they behave in your company. You will also know if the pupils trust you, for example whether they chat to you or ask for advice. However, be careful about courting popularity and remember to be true to your principles and beliefs. I mentioned in Chapter 6 that the prime purpose of the teacher is not to be liked, but to improve the quality of pupils' learning, and this should be done within a climate of mutual respect. Having said all this, if you can both realise this aim and be popular too, what more do you want from your work?

Finally, I want to remind you how much potential influence you have over these young people. Chapters 2 and 4 are a testimony to this. You should look upon your role as a privilege and take your re-sponsibilities seriously. I want to conclude with a story about one of my former pupils. Let's call her Sonia. When Sonia first came into my tutor group, she was a shy little thing with really low self-esteem. Her distinct lack of confidence meant that she was very much affected by the views and opinions of the other children in the class and, as a con-sequence, she made very few autonomous decisions.

Whilst driving the mini-bus back from a Year 7 form trip to a local rolling skating rink, I struck up a conversation with Sonia and her friends. I mentioned how far I felt that she had come over the past year, but then told her that I felt she still needed to take a lot more risks. She wholeheartedly agreed with this. Then, in jest, I gave her the following challenge. During the leavers' assembly in Year 11, she was to put on a pair of Wellington boots, walk on to the stage in front of the three hundred or so pupils, and then place a bucket over her head. We all laughed at the idea and I then forgot about our conversation.

Well, you've guessed it! Four years later, I was standing at the back of the hall during the leavers' assembly, when the head of year announced that Sonia had got a surprise for Mr Dixie. To my astonishment and great pride, up walked Sonia in her Wellington boots with bucket in hand. She made her way to the centre of the stage, and in a loud, confident and assertive voice, informed the audience of the challenge I had offered her four years previously. With that, she picked up the bucket and placed it firmly on her head. She left the stage to the rapturous applause of the audience. This was one of my proudest moments in teaching! I hope that the strategies offered in this book enable you to experience many such moments.

No one has yet realized the wealth of sympathy, the kindness and generosity hidden in the soul of a child. The effort of every true education should be to unlock that treasure. (Emma Goldman)

If you would like to contact me about any of the issues raised in the book then please e-mail me at gererddixie@aol.com. I will do my best to send you a reply.

Bibliography

Barnes, D. (1979) "Language in the secondary classroom" in D. Barnes, J. Britton and H. Rosen (eds) *Language, the Learner and the School*. Harmondsworth: Penguin.

Cooley, C.H. (1902) *Human Nature and Social Order*. New York: Scribner.

Dixie, G. (1998) "Free speech", *TES*, 23rd October.

Dixie, G. (2000) "A room you can call your own", *TES*, 27th October.

Dixie, G. (2003) *Managing Your Classroom*. London: Continuum.

Furlong, J. and Maynard, T. (1995) *Mentoring Student Teachers*. London: Routledge.

Humphreys, T. (1995) *A Different Kind of Teacher*. London: Cassell.

Kaplan, Louise J. (1984) *Adolescence, the Farewell to Childhood*. New York: Simon and Schuster.

Keddie, N. (1976) *Tinker, Taylor … the Myth of Cultural Deprivation*. Harmonsworth: Penguin.

Kutnik, P. and Jules, V. (1988) "Pupils' perceptions of a good teacher: a developmental perspective from Trinida and Tobago", unpublished research, Sussex University.

Kyriacou, C. (2001) *Effective Teaching in Schools*. Cheltenham: Nelson Thornes.

Kyriacou, C. and Cheng, H. (1993) "Student teachers' attitudes towards the humanistic approach to teaching and learning in schools", *European Journal of Teacher Education*, 16, 163-8.

Lewin, K., Lippitt, R. and White, R. (1939) "Patterns of aggressive behaviour in experimentally created 'social climates' ", *Journal of Social Psychology*, 10, 271-99.

Marsh, P., Rosser, E. and Harre, R. (1978) *The Rules of Disorder.* London: Routledge and Kegan Paul.

Mitchell, L. (1996) "The effects of waiting time on excluded children" in E. Blyth and J. Milner (eds) *Exclusion from School: interprofessional issues for policy and practice.* London: Routledge.

National Union of Teachers (2000) "Unacceptable pupil behaviour", *NUT News 28*, 3rd November.

Olsen, J. and Cooper, P. (2002) *Dealing with Disruptive Students in the Classroom.* London: *TES*: Kogan Page.

Phinn, G. (2001) *It Takes One to Know One.* London: Puffin.

Rist, R. (1970) "Student social class and teacher expectations: the self-fulfilling prophecy in ghetto educations", *Harvard Educational Review*, 40.

Rogers, B. (1998) *You Know the Fair Rule.* London: Pitman.

Shaw, S. and Hawes, T. (1998) *Effective Teaching and Learning in the Primary Classroom.* Leicester: Optimal Learning.

Taylor, P. (1962) "Children's evaluation of the characteristics of a good teacher", *British Journal of Educational Psychology*, 32, 258-66.

Ward, J. (1926) *Psychology Applied to Education, Lectures Given at Cambridge in 1880.* Cambridge: Cambridge University Press.

Wragg, T. (1984) *Classroom Teaching Skills: research findings of the teacher education project.* London: Croom Helm.

Zimpher, N. and Howey, K. (1987) "Adapting supervisory practices to different orientations of teaching competence", *Journal of Curriculum and Supervision*, Winter, 2, 104 -7.